Reviewers praise WHY CATHOLIC?

"If this book has any lasting value, it is that it gives a faithful exposition of the attitudes of various articulate Catholics toward their faith in the post-Vatican II period." —*National Catholic Register*

"The responses of these nine must throw a good deal of light on why there are 50 million American Catholics. . . . It may be that those 50 million Catholics know something about life that I'm not strong enough to face." —Jack Beatty in *New Republic*

"Since each essay in *Why Catholic?* reflects the unique personal history, temperament, and theological stance of the writer, the collection offers a wide sampling of the variety of Roman Catholic attitudes towards the institutional Church . . . this book may develop renewed awareness of the strengths of an institution whose faults we recently have been only too eager to habitually spotlight." —*The New Review of Books and Religion*

". . . a surprising unanimity is to be found in these pages. Hardly one of them fails to mention the great cultural and intellectual heritage the Church offers." —*Catholic Review*

"Surely this is a welcome book . . . insightful and worthwhile reading." —*Best Sellers*

". . . substantial, provocative professions of faith, blended with autobiographical details of some rather exciting people . . . their personal faith-stories are reassuring." —*Spiritual Book News*

"*Why Catholic?* gives us yet another reason to be grateful to Mr. Delaney. The 'father' of the famed Image Books, he is probably responsible for keeping more people in the Church than a score of mission bands." —*The Critic*

"Catholic readers who have perhaps put the question, 'why Catholic?' to themselves in recent years, as well as those who find others —including their own children—asking it of them, will be informed, stimulated, and encouraged by the range and diversity of what these Catholic authors have to say." —*U.S. Catholic*

WHY CATHOLIC?

WHY
CATHOLIC?

Complete and Unabridged

John J. Delaney, editor

IMAGE BOOKS

A Division of Doubleday & Company, Inc.
Garden City, New York
1980

Image Book Edition published March 1980
by special arrangement with
Doubleday & Company, Inc.

ISBN: 0-385-14185-8

To
Ann
and
Dan Herr
for their loving friendship over these many years

CONTENTS

FOREWORD

John J. Delaney

And know that I am with you always;
yes, to the end of time.

Matt. 28:20

The changes and upheavals that have characterized life in the Catholic Church in the past decade and a half have shaken the faith of many who regarded the Church as the one element of stability in a chaotic age. Not only were age-old customs and practices discarded, but even dogmas long since defined and considered basic to Catholic belief were being questioned and challenged.

The mass exodus of religious from their ministries and the decline in Mass attendance and church activities added another ominous note to the foreboding and gave those prophets of gloom proclaiming the demise of yet another venerable institution added fuel for their forecasts. Thousands of priests and tens of thousands of nuns left their churches and convents. The decline in weekly Mass attendance in the United States from 71 per cent to 50 per cent in the period 1963 to 1974 according to the sociological data in *Catholic Schools in a Declining Church* is one example of the depressing statistics revealing the serious condition the Church was in.

And all of the foregoing is, unhappily, true and has been headlined in books and newspaper and magazine articles both secular and religious. To many, the conclusions to be drawn were only too obvious—the Catholic Church was in the last stages of its long life.

But there is another side to the matter. It is a fact that thousands of priests have left their ministries, but according to the latest available statistics (*Official Catholic Directory* 1978) there are 58,485 priests still serving the Church in the United States. Tens of thousands of nuns have abandoned their sisterhoods but there are 129,391 still serving. And the Catholic population is listed as 49,836,176. Also, it seems to me, of great significance is the report in *Catholic Schools in a Declining Church* that the number of communicants increased from 20 per cent of those attending Mass to more than 50 per cent in the years covered.

Why? If the Church is a dying institution, why are there still so many priests, nuns, and lay people professing Catholicism as their religion? What is it that is keeping these people in the Church? Surely something more than sheer inertia is at work. What are the operative factors that cause millions to continue practicing their Catholic faith in the face of all the ferment, discontent, and change that is taking place?

It was in an attempt to answer this basic question of why one is a Catholic that I asked the eight authors represented in this book to articulate their belief, to explain why they are Catholics. They cover a wide spectrum in their approaches, but each professes his or her Catholicism and explains why. Each does so in a highly personal way, but it is interesting to note the several uniform themes which run through each of the articles.

It is my hope that these expressions of belief by a distinguished group of men and women will be of help to their fellow Catholics as we grope our way through these trying times in quest of the Eternal Perfection which awaits us all.

J.J.D.

MID-LIFE CONFESSIONS
OF A CATHOLIC

SIDNEY CALLAHAN

Born in Washington, D.C., Sidney Callahan received her B.A. *summa cum laude* from Bryn Mawr and her M.A. from Sarah Lawrence, and is a doctoral candidate at C.U.N.Y. She has received several honorary degrees and awards, is assistant professor of psychology at Fairfield University Graduate School of Education, and serves on many national boards and committees. She has lectured at some 150 colleges, has made many TV appearances, and has written articles for such magazines as *The Critic, The National Catholic Reporter, Commonweal, The New Republic, The Christian Century,* and *Theological Studies.* She has contributed essays to more than a dozen books and is the author of several books, among them *The Illusion of Eve* and *Parenting.* She is married to Daniel Callahan, Director of the Institute of Society, Ethics, and the Life Sciences, and they have six children.

I am a Catholic because I give a real assent to the claims of the Roman Catholic Church to be the fullest, most explicit way to be one with Jesus, God, and the Holy Spirit. I believe the basic doctrines, I want to be in communion with Catholics present and past, and I want to worship and pray as a Roman Catholic. In fact, I can't manage any other way of being a Christian. Nor can I succeed in being an unbeliever, for no matter how high the tide of my doubt rises, it never covers the rock. I am always left standing to get on with the business of a Christian life, and with no excuses.

Perhaps we have the questions all wrong anyway. Instead of asking, "Why Catholic?" it might be more appropriate to ask, "Why Not Catholic?" Surely in the long worshiping history of the human species, it is unbelief which is the unusual condition. Even within recorded time, spasms of secularism or scientism never seem to last long. After a period of atheism there's usually some rebound and deluge of superfaith, complete with true believers glorying in their irrational acceptance of the absurd. Young people in the various cults of today are an example of zealous reaction to secularism. Are Savonarola and Sun Myung Moon so very different?

With middle-aged historical perspective I can now see my own youthful "conversion," first to adult Christianity and then to Roman Catholicism, in a much less individualistic light. Mostly I was returning in reaction to the faith of my forebears: generations upon generations of Baptists and Presbyterians and Methodists who poured into the southern regions of America in the name of religious freedom and secular opportunity. They were farmers, ministers, teachers, craftsmen, and surveyors when they weren't fighting wars. Only after the First World War, during the roaring twenties, had my parents come north and lapsed from the faith. They were still embued with their own childhood Calvinist Christianity, but they did not practice beyond an occasional Easter sunrise service. If you didn't have to go inside a church, it was all right to worship. My father in particular was a believer in science and the march of progress; he also harbored bitter feelings toward the hypocrisies of the small-town Alabama Christians he had known. Mothers in my world generally went along with fathers, at least in overt behavior.

Back home in the South, many of the males among our relatives were skeptical, but the women, one and all, were devout believers. They prayed, read the Bible, went to church twice on Sunday, taught Sunday School, played the organ, sang in the choir, and were even deaconesses in their congregations when that was allowed. The faith of the women seemed to war against the tendency of the men to break the stringent rules, especially the temperance taboo against whiskey. On one side of my family, among the fervent Primitive Baptists, everything seemed to be against the rules: cards, dancing, reading magazines, and of course by implication, sex.

When I hear born Catholics talk about the repressiveness of their upbringing, I smile. They are amateurs at feeling sinful, guilty, and suppressed. From the rigidity of Protestantism my parents had fled north to freedom. But even in my parents' drinking, partying, dancing, card-playing household a certain puritanical judgment of others remained. They were suspicious of all Northerners' morals and particularly shocked at Roman Catholics with their loose ways and sexual waywardness. After all, as everyone knew, Catholics could go to confession and then go right back out and sin again! Filled with superstition and corrupt to the core, Catholics were a group you couldn't help despising and pitying a bit. Of course, occasionally one's third-best friends might be Catholic

—and then there was always Bing Crosby, in his real life and in the movies. The point was that while my parents were ambivalent, living a good Christian life was still an ideal system in which we swam.

I've often wondered whether my Alabama aunts and our black Alabama maids were the ones responsible for my earliest memories of a sense of love, wonder, awe, and worshipfulness. Or maybe all children feel this way and then forget it. At any rate there was a believing loving feminine network which sustained me through the early loss of my mother. My sister and I were left in our young adored father's care. We were partly poor babes in the woods and partly little petted princesses. Perhaps it is the experience of dealing with the idea of death at an early age which produces a sharpened sense of self-consciousness and spiritual awareness. The radical discontinuity awakens in the child the realization that there is something beyond the ordinary daily round of superficial happenings. What is the hidden reality? How exciting to be alive, seeking to know, and to sing our first song, "Jesus loves me, this I know, for the Bible tells me so." Who taught me this, and my other bedtime prayers?

Another death in the family was also significant in my childhood quest for understanding and sense of mystery. My young Uncle Jack had been killed in an air race before I was born. He had gone to the Naval Academy and been a member of the Navy's Blue Devils team. My father loved Jack and always saluted his memory when we drove by the National Cemetery on the way to our home in Arlington. Watching this gesture and seeing the reverence we had for Jack's sword and medals, I would ponder and meditate on the meaning of death. Where was heaven? Where was Uncle Jack now, and where was my mother? Somehow I felt the Bible had the answer; I used to look at Jack's Bible from the Naval Academy and wish I could understand it. With the greatest of care and superstition we never committed the sacrilege of putting any other book on top of a Bible. Bibles had taboo and power associated with them.

Obviously, while I wasn't being formally instructed or sent

to Sunday School, I was certainly primed to hear the word. And in the 1940s, when I was in the fifth grade, a lovely woman came to teach us religion in our tiny two-room schoolhouse perched on Arlington Ridge overlooking the city of Washington. Despite the separation of church and state, Virginia in those days had daily prayers and Bible reading in the morning along with the flag salute and "My country, 'tis of thee." Also at this time the Second World War was raging and life seemed very serious and full of drama, conflict, and the possibility of death and suffering. My Uncle Tom, who had gone to West Point, was fighting in Europe, and my father went back into the Navy. We had an English refugee child living with us for a while and heard firsthand of death from the skies, on the seas, and, of course, in our friends' families, who almost all had members in the Army and the Navy. Stories of Nazi and Japanese atrocities were regularly appearing in the papers and on the radio.

In the midst of this our religion teacher seemed unafraid and openly talked to us about death and our fear of death. She stressed the good news of the Resurrection and told us how much God loved each one of us. (The two Catholic children in school were excused and sat upstairs while this was going on.) Our teacher also told us that we ought to go to Sunday School regularly. We had to make charts in our notebooks for each Sunday of the month, and if we attended Sunday School, we could draw a picture in the empty space. I think we also got gold stars or butterfly stickers to paste in. Entranced by this teacher, whose name I can't remember, and never one to refrain from chasing gold stars, I began to go to Methodist Sunday School with my best friend. It was a whole lot farther down the hill than the Baptist church, but I had once been to the Baptist church with another friend and found the idea of total immersion under water totally frightening. Besides my fear of the baptismal rite, I also felt averse to the Baptists' strict requirement that you attend the adult worship service every Sunday. Such boredom was beyond me, and at the Methodist church our ineffectual, good-hearted teachers were satisfied by an occasional attendance at the worship service. In Sunday School I was my usual achieving self and a model little girl of great seriousness. I could barely tolerate the boisterous boys who kept the class in chaos, and I felt pity for our teachers.

At home, the attitude toward my Sunday School going was kind toleration. The only injunction from my father was, "You can go if you want, but once you begin, you have to finish." Finishing things is of course the hardest thing to do, and personal character was more important at home than religious talk. For me this was and is a home truth; I am engaged in an internal struggle to conquer sloth, to put my desire to be good and disciplined above my desire for pleasure and ease. How tempted I was at times to skip Sunday School, lie, and still get my gold star in a beautiful notebook. At the same time, how virtuous I felt, getting up Sundays by myself, picking my way through the remains of my parents' Saturday-night party and walking a mile to church all alone. On these occasions I always felt close to God and got something out of it, despite the rowdy boys and boring talks. I was seeking truth, love, and understanding and struggling to master my undisciplined childish self.

At this point in the war, the Navy transferred us around rapidly and I went to three schools in the sixth grade. Only one Sunday School experience in all of this moving stands out —a Presbyterian Sunday School in New Orleans. In Louisiana I was in the minority as a Protestant, and when a bell rang, all the Catholics left school for released-time instruction and three Protestants were left behind in class. I quickly found a best friend and went to Sunday School with her, gaining gold stars this time for memorizing all the books of the Bible and learning my lessons. There was no rowdiness and the classes and services seemed more intellectual and organized. I liked it, and can see with hindsight that I was responding to the greater degree of structure. But we soon left for home, and in Arlington again I joined the Methodist Church in the seventh grade on Christmas Eve. I felt close to God and very grown up. I also discovered in the formal proceedings of filling out forms that I had been baptized before. My unknown mother had had me baptized in the Episcopal Church in the Bethlehem Chapel of the National Cathedral. In a Graham Greene novel, that early baptism would account for my childhood faith rather than any influence of Alabama relatives or early bereavement.

When the Second World War finally ended, we moved once again, into the city of Washington. It was exciting to live in a city, and my sister and I took a turn at Sunday School and the junior choir in the nearby First Baptist Church, where Jimmy Carter now goes. Here in the throes of early adolescence at fourteen my struggle with discipline broke down completely; boredom and sloth conquered. I didn't care, dropped out, and went back to the dissipation of sleep on Sundays, despite my enthusiasm for books like Lloyd Douglas's *The Robe* and Pearl Buck's tales of her missionary parents in China.

When two or three more years had passed, my father went to sea again. With his disapproving presence removed, my stepmother investigated a new church which had opened in a townhouse right around the corner from our house. This turned out to be the notable Church of the Savior, of which much has been written. The founders were young attractive adventurous Southerners who were risking all for the love of Jesus Christ. They advocated an ecumenical Christian life of disciplined commitment of money, time, work, prayer, and intellectual study. There was a beauty and restrained fervor in the worship and an exciting social fellowship in the tiny church-in-a-house.

As a teen-ager among young adults I was attracted, skeptical, but finally convinced that prayer and a mystical life combined with good works were a real possibility for modern people. One could be rational, sophisticated, aesthetic, social, witty, and also a devoted believer. I count my life as an adult Christian as beginning with that band of gracious followers of the Lord. They fanned the dying coals of my childhood faith into a crackling flame. As a young church member I was introduced to Christian classics I had not even known existed. I read C. S. Lewis, *The Imitation of Christ*, St.

Augustine, and of course the Bible over and over, along with commentaries. Engaging in prayer and disciplined devotion gave me a honeymoon feeling of flying and sailing through a life of joy in God's service. This late-adolescent euphoria was heightened by my father's disapproval and the slight disdain for ardent Christianity which reigned at my upper-class private girl's school. How fortunate I was that my adolescent rebellion took the form of enthusiastic discipleship, asceticism, and intellectual seriousness of purpose. After all, in my parents' world one didn't take either religion or the intellectual life *too* seriously.

My radical Christian beliefs also made me open my thinking to many new things. My faith strengthened an incipient tendency toward racial integration and feminism. Once the constraints of my southern military world were loosened, I could even imagine going north to a feminist college like Bryn Mawr. Off I went after winning a partial scholarship and was overjoyed to find a place where it was all right to be an intellectual under my southern-belle exterior. But it wasn't all right in the fifties to be a believing, enthusiastic Christian. Those of us who were, found each other and met in cell groups to pray and read Scripture together. Again it was inspiring to be vaguely disapproved of and scorned for our faith.

Finding an institutional home for my Christianity while at college was more difficult. I went to a nearby Methodist and a nearby Presbyterian church, gave up, and then was deeply moved by and interested in the Quakers. I attended meeting regularly and participated in Quaker work camps in the slums of Philadelphia. But after several years my college studies as an English and history major began to have an effect on my religious quest. During a history course on the Enlightenment I was enlightened as to where my own prejudices against "medieval superstition and priestcraft" had come from. They came straight from the eighteenth century to me via southern Protestantism and my father's belief in progress. Courses in philosophy and poetry led me slowly to a need for a more intellectual, aesthetic, sacramental worship and religious life. I went from the Quakers to the low Episcopal Church, then to the high Anglo-Catholic Episcopal Church, and finally with a struggle burst out of my cocoon into Roman Catholicism.

It wasn't easy to get in during those pre-Vatican II, pre-Pope John days. I had to be rebaptized—in St. Matthew's Cathedral in Washington this time—and sign an assent to everything every Protestant had ever protested against throughout church history. When I came for instruction with my *Commonweal* in hand, I got into an immediate argument with the priest on duty. I told him I came there because the local priest in Bryn Mawr refused to have anything to do with Bryn Mawr girls. Furthermore, I hated the ornate decorations of St. Matthew's and knew that Joe McCarthy went there. My line was that if I could enter the Catholic Church there, at the bottom so to speak, I could always manage anywhere else.

This priest turned out to be McCarthy's great friend and spiritual advisor, so no wonder we had a total nonmeeting of the minds. He quickly decided to turn me over to a delightful old French priest in residence, "another heretic like you." This priest had spent his life in the missions in India and was spiritual, worldly, and wise as well as kind and witty. We agreed on everything, from a devotion to the Spirit to a dismissal of the Index and the various legalisms which used to vex Catholics in those days. We zoomed through instruction, since I'd already read myself into Roman Catholicism à la Newman, and I was received into the Church with a great deal of inner joy.

All the forces and convictions which brought me in keep me in. To me it was like finally coming home, but that feeling has never gone unchallenged for the last twenty-five years. My family were truly horrified in a deep, residually prejudiced way; this was worse than the queer Quaker business or my other radical intellectual and political ideas. And at Bryn Mawr in those days to become a Roman Catholic voluntarily was like volunteering to be a leper. There was one Catholic faculty member, a funny little Italian lady who taught Dante, so she couldn't help it, of course. I adored being even more in a minority than before and found exciting Catholic movements like the Grail and the Catholic Worker Movement to keep me sustained.

Later, when I was married and living in the Harvard Graduate School milieu, where secularism also reigned, Catholics were beleaguered and had to defend themselves against very crude prejudices and misunderstandings. Things were much better after Pope John and the Council, but then a new challenge arose. During the late sixties and early seventies many of my Catholic friends and my immediate family departed the faith. Some burned themselves out, some faded away gracefully, and some harangued and harassed me for hanging in and hanging on. In my world I am condemned to be self-consciously Roman Catholic, and so I am.

Like most of the others I know who remain within the fold, I too have my ups and downs. I have had periods of intensely disciplined, joyful spirituality and periods of lazy, lax scraping by with a minimum of anemic practice. These different religious periods seem correlated with events and conditions in my life as a whole. Take, for example, my first eleven years of marriage. We were fervent followers of the Catholic Worker and the liturgical revival movements and espoused living by providence, hard work, and asceticism. During that time we had seven children, one crib death, no money, ten moves, nine years of graduate school (my husband's Ph.D.) and wrote and published three books (two my husband's, one mine). I felt God was close through every hardship, sorrow, and joy. The next thirteen years brought some struggles with adolescents, one operation, more graduate school (mine), more books (ours), lecture engagements, recognition, much more money, and some security. In these much more stable, easier times my old spiritual sloth would often rise up and overcome me. Middle-age fatigue may have also set in. Or perhaps, as in the case of those who fought wars in their youth, nothing could ever equal the emotional and spiritual intensity of actual emergency conditions. God is near to the poor and those living under great stress, because they need Him so much and have nowhere else to turn for help.

I find it much harder to remain faithful when thoroughly immersed in rewarding intellectual work, a hectic social life, and an older family. In middle-class, middle-aged, affluent sophisticated New York urban culture one has to fight to keep one's Christian ground cleared from the distracting overgrowth of other plants. Again and again the world intrudes with its insistence on success, making a splash, having beautiful things, and giving your children everything. The only counterweight the middle classes have is access to art, music, and beauty. The exaltation brought on by music, ballet, or a great dramatic performance can rekindle the sense of awe and transcendence that can get buried in the everyday rush. Leisure also helps. On the rare occasions when we have been able to go to some quiet, beautiful place near the ocean and there is time for reflection, then I center down once more.

Right now with more leisure I feel on an upswing, contented, and enjoying work and family and faith. This mellowness and happiness restores the spirit. I am returning to old sources of strength: Julian of Norwich, Baron von Hügel, Augustine. As we go through the ever-new cycle of the liturgical year, I am deeply happy and grateful for good fortune, if not ecstatic. I've almost stopped berating myself because I don't get to Holy Days of Obligation and sometimes miss Mass and don't pray regularly. Much as I would love to love heroically, I recognize that I am a mediocre Christian, but that God loves me anyway and can make use of me. It's all right to be average and be among the company of the faithful struggling to do God's will.

Indeed, as I look back over my life I would have to say that belief and faith have never been a problem, but works have been. Even during my less active times in my adolescence I remember believing the basics in a general way. My whole Christian life has always risen and fallen on my willingness to *practice* what I believe. I hate getting up in the morning. I hate giving up comfort, money, time, or my own will. I want things and don't want to have to be concerned for the other people in the world. When I overcome sloth and selfishness by behaving differently, then I flourish. It seems to me that Catholicism perfectly understands the importance of behavior and action for the growth of faith.

Yet at the same time the Church is definitely an inclusive church and not a sect or an elite. There's room for every class, race, style of devotion, and personal temperament. Each country and culture can produce a Catholicism of its own, just as each person at Pentecost heard the word in his or her own language. A Catholic Church should be able to meet everyone where they live in an appropriate and inviting language. A sect or elite group of the saved always imposes, divides, and demands rigid obedience in particulars. You only meet one kind of people in a sect, and when you become a different kind of person, out you go. The Church, no matter what theological model of it you adhere to, cannot negate the other models. An inclusive Church witnesses to the fact that it serves a God who will never "break the crushed reed nor put out the smoldering wick." The people will include those at different stages of development.

The variety of the people involved is also one of the great comforts of being a Catholic. The multitude of saints and heroes and heroines available for emulation opens up your own horizons while giving you a proper modesty and irony. The Catholic past offers everyone from the incredibly attractive Thomas More to the dreadful Curé d'Ars for devotion. You can learn from Joan of Arc, Perpetua and Felicity, or the great Teresa. There are many eccentric ascetic great women of the Church, too, but somehow they don't put me off like their male counterparts do. I guess I excuse their extremism as a reaction to the masculine-dominated culture. At any rate, I am conscious that there they all are—a heroic company of infinite variety united in a tenuous but real way in the barque of Peter.

Present inspirations within the Roman communion also help me. It seems no accident that the people I most admire in the modern world turn out to be Catholics. Cesar Chavez, Dorothy Day, Mother Teresa, to name only a few, are all particularly Catholic in their approach to life. Similarly in the world of the arts I also am attracted to the Catholic and Anglo-Catholic artists who have an inclusive, deeply human perspective. Right now I am finally getting around to reading Dante, and I see the great exemplar of baptizing and incorporating everything admirable in your own synthesis. The fact that Dante put popes in hell also shows a good Catholic attitude toward authority. (I also like the fact that the slothful make it into purgatory.)

It's important to me that the Church has always fostered an intense intellectual and scholarly life. Catholicism is the best religion for an intellectual since rational understanding and scholarship are so highly valued as a way to truth. The light of learning was kept alive through the centuries by the labor of dedicated Christian churchmen. Catholic universities and religious orders have been founded to serve God through the intellectual life. It is an impressive record.

In my own experience my Catholicism led me to expand my intellectual horizons. I read history, theology, and philosophy in order to understand my faith better. I became educated through reading journals such as *Cross-Currents, Commonweal, Theological Studies,* and a host of others. European intellectual life became a reality to me in a way it never was before. When Catholic intellectuals and scholars came over here, I would often have a chance to meet them and be stimulated to more study and thought myself. The ideal of learning and disciplined study is very strong within Catholicism.

All of this study and thinking usually keeps one from becoming a "true believer" and instead produces a healthy skepticism toward new movements. Since Catholics already have a religion, they don't tend to make a religion out of their professional work, psychological processes, or their sex life. Indeed, the balance, irony, and humanism of the Catholic tradition fosters perhaps its most attractive quality—viz., a wonderful wit and humor. Catholics laugh at themselves more than most other groups and seem to find the fun in life with more élan. It may have something to do with Celtic culture, or the presence of drinking, music, and dancing, but Catholics do seem to be among the merriest folk around.

I love being a Catholic because this form of Christianity gives me a larger and more various world, in which nothing which is human is alien. There is plenty of space to move in all directions, especially upwards toward heaven. The Catholic emphasis upon transcendence and mystery helps me through times of doubt, stress, and difficulties. If God is more than whatever we can imagine and the Trinity is a living mystery beyond comprehension, then obviously our grasp on the faith is bound to be fumbling much of the time. As Baron von Hügel and others have noted, considering and comparing the reality of divinity to humankind, we can hardly expect to grasp the truth as though it were a set of clear and distinct propositions. The quality of mystery is quite strained. While we may be sure that we believe, we may not be able to draw the lineaments of the face on which no man may look and live.

At the same time, in the great paradox, Catholic Christianity emphasizes God's accessibility in Jesus and in the indwelling Spirit. In the great Sacrament of the Church we can hear, understand, and live what is necessary. The message is clear enough for our salvation but never comprehensible enough for us to be bored or smug. Within our liturgical life we celebrate. God gives us gifts, we say thank you, and give our gifts back only to have them returned, in an ongoing perpetual exchange of loving kindness. This eternal graciousness at the center of the world we can be sure of and count on, no matter what mysteries or catastrophes may exist on the periphery. The sacramental signs and actions keep us in touch and very down to earth: bread, wine, water, fire, touch—and all accompanied by exchanges of the word. The common Catholic Christian life is very simple, very beautiful, very happy, and very involved with the human body, home, and family.

Recently I participated in an ecumenical consultation with a Christian communion descended from the Calvinist tradition. During the meetings devoted to common ethical issues we took turns providing the morning worship service. On the Catholic morning it happened to be the feast of the Visitation, and during Mass I had a sudden insight. How utterly and completely feminine and familial the Catholic Church is compared to the sterner more austere Protestants. There we all were, celebrating the visit of one pregnant woman to another who happened to be her cousin. We read about babies leaping in the womb for joy and heard recited the glorious magnificat of one of the pregnant women. Then we sang a song in praise of Mary, a mother who delighted in childbirth and the baby.

During the service we were all kneeling and bowing, gesturing, clasping hands and making graceful signs, feeding and being fed in the most expressive way. Even the fact that there were seven priests at the altar concelebrating in unison looked as familial as the constant addresses to "father," "brothers," and "sisters." No wonder people have called the Catholic Church a mother, I thought. In remaining so feminine and motherly it serves as a basic reminder of God as Mother, as well as wrapped in transcendence. I wonder if the babies who regularly turn up on church doorsteps are symbolic of the Catholic Church's insistence on retaining devotion to a loving maternity in all its manifestations. By keeping our Mariology and the cult of the saints we have emphasized the organic fullness of a communion of flesh as well as spirit. A romantic expressiveness and sweetness (ever ready to go too far and become sentimentality and superstition, alas) remains in the Catholic tradition. What some have called the fairy-tale aspect of Christianity hasn't been lost. The child in us is nourished along with the adult.

The Catholic Church's ability simultaneously to symbolize both transcendence and immanence is compelling. How akin I find mysticism and those qualities of worship and life traditionally called feminine. I can now understand why as a young convert I took the name of Mary for my confirmation name, in honor of Our Lady and to symbolize all that I could not get in Protestant faith and worship. In still another way the Catholic Church is the closest I can come to worshiping as freely and joyfully as our black friends did in the churches I visited in my childhood. Now if we could just incorporate dancing and more spontaneity in our liturgy, we could have everything. Perhaps some Catholic Pentecostals are already working on the dancing problem and I don't know it yet.

A few other serious problems remain to be worked on as well. Since for me being Catholic is to recover the feminine and human wholeness, it is deeply disappointing that women are not yet ordained and given access to the hierarchy and formal leadership. Restricting the priesthood to male celibates seems a direct symbolic contradiction of the Catholic emphasis upon community and fullness of life. None of the arguments against married clergy or against female clergy seem cogent or convincing. In the end they mostly seem to be reduced to the argument that we've never done it before. To argue from past human traditions rather than to reason from what God wants for now and the future shows a particularly limited sense of time. The world may exist for a million more years, and it may then be remembered that in the first few seconds of the Church's life it countenanced slavery, and for the first few minutes barred women from ordination, and off and on for a minute or two required celibacy for all the clergy instead of viewing celibacy as a gift of grace.

In the future, too, Catholics will need better leadership to represent and minister more fully to all the people. If the future is short and we are on the way to the day of judgment, then all the more reason to be living by the Kingdom's revolutionary ways of including all equally rather than by an outmoded partriarchal system. Practically speaking, with women and married people in leadership roles, the Church may be saved from more blunders in the realm of sexuality and marriage. Since I think Catholics have the right basic ideas about sex, I cringe when we seem to obscure our message with irrelevant prohibitions. Protection of the helpless preborn seems as important as protecting the old, the poor, the sick, and other powerless groups. But protecting the integrity of a body's reproductive cycle or fertility seems a misplaced biologism and nature mystique.

It is not ever easy to get the proper balance in our exercise of Christian stewardship over nature. To go too far in dominion and control produces ecological disasters in both the physical and the psychological realm. To go too far in passivity and letting be what will be produces even more evil. In the past many Catholics have been guilty of what I can only call a pathology of hope, or too much trust, too soon, for too long. To practice proper discernment about the difficult questions we are going to face, we need a leader who can be more in touch with the world, with themselves, and with the people they serve. At this point many, many Catholics who are enthusiastic and devoted members of the Catholic worship community and intellectual community receive many of the pronouncements of authority as though they came from a distant, distant galaxy. In my own case I feel I am in the same galaxy with the hierarchy, even in the same orbit, but not usually on the same planet.

To use a more biblical image, a shepherd will not be able to call the sheep and have them follow unless the sheep feel the shepherd loves and understands them. Jesus is the Good Shepherd because he is tender, loving, and terribly effective. He could make his followers' hearts burn within them and at the same time speak of transcendent and mysterious truths. Great Christian pastors do the same. And it does seem that things go so much better with the Church when our great Christian leaders are comfortably within the authority structures rather than being harassed, hounded, or ignored. Opening up the available pool of possible priests and bishops and letting more people get involved in their selection is a first and long-overdue step. I've long been making a list of good candidates for the first women bishops: women such as Mary Perkins Ryan, Rosemary Haughton, and Sister Anita Caspery, among others. Sister Anita is only one of many superb women religious leaders in the United States. In my opinion the orders of sisters in this country should be proud indeed of their members; so often they are the best models around of what a twenty-first-century Catholic can be like.

As American Catholics approaching the twenty-first century become more and more assimilated, we will face the challenge of acceptance and affluence, always more difficult than being scorned and persecuted for Christ. Yes there is still a lot of anti-Catholicism in this country, as the abortion debate has revealed. But slowly the last bastions of power and prestige are falling. Any day now there may be a Catholic president of Harvard (much more difficult to have than a Catholic President of the United States) or a Catholic heading the Ford or Rockefeller Foundation. Women and Catholics are slowly making it; and when a Catholic woman like Ella Grasso is the first woman elected on her own as governor of a state, it's an auspicious sign.

I myself was particularly honored and happy to be asked to be the first woman to give the baccalaureate address at Columbia University. The three major religions rotate the right to invite the speaker and 1978 was the Catholics' turn. I think it typical that the Catholics were the first to ask a woman. I also was happy in surveying the scene to note that a woman was president of Barnard, so that now women head every one of the Seven Sisters colleges. As for Columbia, both the president and vice-president are Catholics as well as a large proportion of the students. This is a definite change from the recent past.

Since this year's baccalaureate service took place on Pentecost and Mother's Day, I had a ready-made theme. I could speak for feminism, family life, and the need to listen to the Spirit when deciding what to do with our lives. I could also stress the much-overlooked but very Catholic consciousness of the motherly aspect of God who promises that in the end every tear will be wiped away and joy will reign. Despite our difficulties, depressions, and trials we are made for happiness and the marriage feast of the Lamb in the New Jerusalem. I think I witness to my Catholic Christianity when I recall these things and remember always that "the Spirit and the Bride say, 'Come'. . . . Then let all who are thirsty come: all who want it may have the water of life, and have it free." Rejoice and be glad in the Lord.

WHY CATHOLIC? WHY NOT?

Born in Worcester, Massachusetts, John Deedy holds degrees from Holy Cross and from Trinity College, Dublin. He was a reporter and correspondent for daily newspapers in Worcester and Boston and beginning in 1951 devoted himself to religious journalism. He was editor of the Worcester diocesan paper, the *Catholic Free Press*, in 1951–59 and of the Pittsburgh diocesan paper, the *Pittsburgh Catholic*, in 1959–67. He became managing editor of *Commonweal* in 1967, writes a column for *Commonweal*, has authored and edited several books, and has contributed articles to the New York *Times*, *The Critic*, *The New Republic*, and other journals.

Twenty-five years in Catholic journalism notwithstanding, I have never found it easy to talk about belief, mine or anyone else's. I have covered religious events from the most inconsequential to the most exalted—from Holy Name Society meetings to a worldwide Ecumenical Council. I have covered religious pilgrimages, lectures, happenings, conventions. No trouble. I have always found it easy to deal with facts and events: the spoken word, the action observed, the deed done. Handling the observed has, in some ways, been but a kind of reflex action. Get the facts straight, the names correct, the details accurate. Easy. The type of reporting I did most of the time as a Catholic journalist didn't require the peeling back of the skin and the examination of the core element that motivated individuals and energized events. Lucky for me. Even at the Second Vatican Council, the professional challenge for me was the sorting out of facts and the ecclesiastical politics of what was taking place. I was there as a reporting journalist, not as a dealer in opinion and motives. That kind of journalist doesn't have to be a diviner, a caseworker. More to the point, he isn't judge and jury. I wasn't, and was happy not to be.

Maybe I created a special kind of professional category for myself and a condition special to religious journalism. I'll let others decide that. Let me say this much: A religious journalist can report on events in a manner similar to the secular journalist; he can take an adversary position on behalf of cause or principle. But he cannot be judgmental in the way that secular journalists might be on occasion. Certainly the religious journalist can go beyond the elementary who, what, where, when, and why of a story. He may interpret. He may editorialize, within limits. He may convey compassion or enthusiasm or other types of feelings. But he cannot be judgmental—indeed, must be very circumspect—on the element that is individually and collectively the central point of religious journalism: belief. Belief is so nuanced a thing, so complex, so personal, so much the inner self that it is presumptuous to be making readings on it. Belief cannot be laid bare, dissected, analyzed, as a political election or Super Bowl game might. I have never thought it could, and have been wary of doing so throughout my career in religious journalism.

Astonishingly, I discover in approaching this essay that it is equally difficult to deal with the belief that is my own. Am I the victim of my trade as I devised it for myself?

It is a curious thing about religious journalism when practiced in the mode conceptualized. One can be an agnostic, a skeptic, a complete atheist even, and—allowing that one is able to live with the dichotomies—still be competent and effective as a religious journalist. I have worked with journalists in the religious press who, if they themselves were to be believed, had as much belief as a squirrel. Wait; this isn't to be judgmental about any one of them (their number isn't large). It is only to accept at face value their readings of themselves. Many were top-notch religious journalists. Why not? One doesn't have to subscribe to the Nicene Creed to interview a cardinal, cover a council, write a pope's obituary, much less report on a meeting of the Diocesan League of Catholic Women. That most religious journalists are believers isn't a coincidence of occupation, but belief isn't a *sine qua non* either. Belief, for instance, had nothing to do with my leaving daily journalism for the religious press. I didn't enter religious journalism as a disciple of anyone or anything. I didn't enter it to save the world or witness to something special. The job looked interesting, and it paid more than I was making in secular journalism. I took it—and my belief survived.

In some respects I may have been lucky. I escaped the close-up look without becoming jaded, without being reduced to cynic and debunker—an occupational hazard for anyone who works up close to almost anything. Look at the books of former workers in the White House. The same risks apply in working for the Church, and they deserve mention because cynicism and negativisms can affect belief. I had a friend—he died a few years ago—whose belief was being constantly shaken by a job he held at a high level in the old National Catholic Welfare Conference in Washington, D.C. "It's better to see the play from the audience rather than the wings," he used to say. My friend built up layers of cynicism about organized religion, if not about faith, and these washed away only after several years in a diffierent job for a totally different organization. He went to work for the government, but he was a long way from the wings; he had a low-level position, and he was happier by far than when he was next to the main stage. Maybe my friend and I are special cases, but I notice that the director of the Christophers, Father John T. Catoir, was warning Catholic journalists at the 1978 Catholic Press Association Convention in San Diego against the pitfall I congratulate myself on escaping. "You have to have a rare kind of wisdom and a deep faith to keep from slipping into cynicism, the last refuge of the disillusioned idealist," Father Catoir commented. "It's bad enough if you work in a rectory; it's worse if you work in the chancery office. But if you work for a Catholic newspaper, where you come across all the news that's unfit to print and in order to survive you have to deal with bishops, pastors, and priests in general, you might have some trouble maintaining the fresh ideals of your youth. The Church can be at times so poor in virtue, so riddled with mediocrity, that she shocks us." He might have added that this Church can also test one's belief.

Going to work for *Commonweal* at the time I did certainly spared my belief, at least such as I carry within me. I was a long time in diocesan Catholic journalism—fifteen years—and maybe that was just long enough. Certainly I got out when the going was good. I got out just before the old institution began to come apart and the organized Church became, if only for a time, an unhappy place of recrimination and abrasion. I could have been turned into cynic with probable chipping of faith and belief, by much of what was occurring. Better to have been at *Commonweal*, where one could intellectualize about events rather than apologize for them or, worse yet, explain them away, the impossible task assumed by some respected old colleagues. *Commonweal* may not have fortified faith and belief, but it helped me keep my Catholicism by sparing my mind some of the cluttering debris of institutionalism. At the very least I was spared the disillusionments that drove some others to what I consider to be acts of folly, including the shedding of their Catholicism.

Still, at *Commonweal*—eleven years—one thing did not change. I forever found it easier to editorialize about the arms race, say, than about faith and belief. A hang-up from my days in diocesan journalism maybe, but so it is—or was; I will have left the magazine by the time this essay is published. I suffered a quiet dread each December that I might have to write the meditative, spiritual editorial that runs in the Christmas issue. Each year I managed to duck it. What relief!

All of which is prelude to the confession—by now readily surmisable—that I didn't even know where to begin this essay —or how—on why I am a Catholic. I made a hundred starts, it seems, and abandoned them one after the other because I sounded so fraudulently pious to myself. For a time I even wondered whether I could get the essay written. Then along came the showing on television of the movie *Nashville*. Now I beg your pardon for coupling the dimensions of religious belief—denominational affiliation, really—with a popular Hollywood movie. But if one generation of American Catholics could get a spiritual uplift from *The Song of Bernadette* or, God help us!, *Going My Way*, then why couldn't I get an idea or clarification of a special religious sort from *Nashville*? Not that I watched the film with anything so lofty in mind. I

watched it for mere diversion—and a light came on. Let me
warn you, this is a dim light and it puts my Catholicism in
superficial focus. Also, an unintellectual focus. And maybe I
shouldn't confess it, but this is the way I got my handle on
my Catholicism.

I was in bed. The television was on. The station break
came, and *Nashville* rolled with a screen character named
Haven Hamilton (Henry Gibson) singing an anthem to
America. The time setting was the Bicentennial, and the
catch phrase of the song was the line "We must be doing
something right to last two hundred years." Of course the
film became a parody of the sentiment, what with the incessant babble, the moral and intellectual chaos, and the ultimate American travesty, an assassination scene. Still it was a
wonderfully diverting film, and for me it was more. I found I
could not chase Haven Hamilton's two-hundred-year phrase
from my mind. It made me think:

Two hundred years of America. What's that when compared with the Catholic Church's two thousand years? And if
a country can be conceded the benefits of longevity—love,
loyalty, respect, credibility—for two hundred years, why not a
Church for two thousand years? It was something to ponder,
though not ponderously, during the commercials. *Nashville*
was parodying the Bicentennial; the birthday king was being
mocked. Hasn't history, I asked myself, often parodied the
Church? Hasn't the Church often been mocked? And as the
country was having the last laugh on *Nashville*, really—it's
still around, and where's the film—hasn't the Church survived
its critics, its travails? Haven Hamilton could have been singing of the babble and chaos in the Church, but do babble
and chaos make the Church any less valid an institution,
and, to the extent that they might, do the two thousand
years count for nothing? I'll go with longevity, I said to myself, and I'll take the babble and the chaos if I have to. After
all, we Catholics weren't promised a rose garden, so why
should we expect one? We were merely promised a Church
that would endure to the end of time. So ungarlanded a
promise carries with it the implicit warning of distracting in-

terruptions in the sweet, free flow of events. Whatever, as I watched *Nashville*, I decided that if two hundred years helped me take America, two thousand years most certainly helped me take Catholicism. It's the shallowest of reasons for being Catholic, very likely, but there it is.

Reason two for being Catholic is probably no more inspiring or convincing. I am a Catholic because I could no more not be a Catholic than I could not be a Deedy or an Irish-American. Catholicism is a part of me, as much as heritage and citizenship are, and maybe even more by making claims on not only my mortality but also my immortality. Catholicism is as much a part of me even as the limbs of my body. It is, in a word, a part of my essential self. I could no more cut it away and feel the same person than I could lop off a limb and not be aware that something vital has been severed from my person.

Why Catholic? Because I could not be other than Catholic and still be who I am. I was born to Catholicism. I like being Catholic—and as I would not choose otherwise for my nationality, I will not choose otherwise for my religious affiliation.

This is not to say that my Catholicism has been an unchanged and unchanging thing throughout my life. Quite the opposite—and that's one of the seductions about Catholicism: It has room for all sorts, its frequently annoying rigidities notwithstanding. Like most Catholics, I have been through several evolutions. There was the literal Catholicism of youth, when not even a St. Philomena was to be doubted. There was the fashionable Pascalianism of early adulthood, when I was willing to take Pascal's wager on the existence of God, figuring, like Pascal, that I had everything to win and, at worst, nothing to lose if it proved out that there was no God up there after all. There was the formalism of what might be called parental Catholicism, when it seemed more important to set an example of belief and worship for the children than to be a genuine believer myself. There was, too, the Catholicism of activism and engagement when the

Church was being remade after Vatican II, and when so many of us were discovering (or rediscovering) the relevance of Catholicism in the combined contexts of a theology of hope, of liberation, of individual freedom. It was a time when encounters with Dorothy Day on behalf of the poor, or Daniel Berrigan on behalf of peace, were worth a dozen Masses and a score of sermons. I thrilled then at being Catholic. More recently there is the Catholicism of cooled ardor, a sign maybe that the fires of life are burning with less heat. In any case I am in a period where I prefer a private and complacent Catholicism.

It's not that I do not want to be challenged any more; it is rather that I want to savor my Catholicism for a while. The soldier has his R&R, his rest and recreation. As Catholic, I'll take my time of R&R—reflection and reserve. This sounds like a Catholicism of resignation and default, but I don't regard it as such. A time of meditation and deactivization may indeed be good for the soul at this stage of my life. And if this is a temporary lapse into formalism, then so be it. I have the consolation of knowing that I'm not the only one of my age group in this category. I had lunch recently in New York with a prominent American, a Catholic. The conversation got around to religion and the old rituals of Catholicism. "Do you bother with them any more?" was the question. "Listen," said the friend, "I've come this far. I'm not going to be shot down by a legalism." There was an intended humor to the remark, but very likely an underlying note of seriousness as well. My status isn't my friend's, but I can understand his attitude. Where we differ is that I actually enjoy the formalities of faith. It is no penance for me to get to Mass every Sunday, to observe the fast and abstinence regulations, and to do whatever else the Church demands of me. If anything, the Church asks too little of me, particularly in terms of all that it makes possible.

In this context let me say that I am a Catholic because I also happen to value the Church as refuge and consolation in times of trouble and distress. The Church, in a way, is my safety valve to anxieties. Go ahead; say it. This makes of my religion nothing more than what Marx said religion was: the opium of the people. Well, maybe it is for me at least part of the time. But we all need our safety valves and I'll take mine, without apology or embarrassment, in Catholicism, its rituals and its prayers. The poet John Fandel once wrote that we are more likely to pray in our misery than in our joy—that an ingrown toenail makes us more aware of God than a starry night. He's so right. And maybe one reason is the Church's special orientation, its reflection of life's travails and crises, and its unique lesson of the triumph that is in tragedy and seemingly utter defeat. There could have been no Resurrection without the Passion, and for me there is no easy meeting of life's trials without the Church of the Cross. I can understand my problems better because of the Church's history of triumph over adversity, and I can cope better with life by having the reservoirs of Catholicism to draw upon.

Now don't misunderstand me. I am not a Catholic by mere accident of birth, nor am I a Catholic because of psychological construction and needs—not solely, not principally. Those may be elements in my Catholicism, but basically I am a Catholic by intellectual choice and persuasion. I am a Catholic because I believe in God. I am a Catholic because I believe this God intervened in history through his Son, Jesus Christ. I am a Catholic because I believe that Jesus Christ founded a Church. I am a Catholic because, whatever claims on validity other Christian churches do have, I believe the Catholic Church to be uniquely the Church of Jesus Christ and of God the Father. Likewise I am a Catholic because, like Malcolm Muggeridge, the British writer and social critic, I find it preposterous to suppose that the universe was set up solely to provide a *mise en scène* for what Muggeridge labels "the interminable soap opera of history, with its stock characters and situations endlessly repeated." In other words I believe in life after death. By the same token, I believe that the satisfactions of the afterlife are contingent on a life lived with merit on this earth.

This last admission moves me, I suppose, toward the category of the selfish or the avaricious, but let me say that I am not avaricious or covetous of eternal reward in the manner, say, of Fräulein Teta Linek in Franz Werfel's novel *Embezzled Heaven* or of William Ferraro in Graham Greene's short story "Special Duties." They were a scheming, calculating pair who sought, respectively, to buy up favor with the Lord and to store up indulgences as a hedge against time in purgatory. I went through my purgatory phase, when a prayer that gained me seven years was to be preferred to one that returned seven quarantines. What middle-aged Catholic hasn't? But I am not a Teta Linek or a William Ferraro, and never was. To be specific, I do not count myself a Catholic out of simple selfish expectancy. If there are rewards in the afterlife, fine; I'll count myself blessed. However, I like to think I am a Catholic for more altruistic reasons—because I can witness to the good of the Father and the values of belief through the Catholic Church better than through another church or no church at all. I speak of the values of the Ten Commandments and of the Gospel messages, notably the Sermon on the Mount.

These values are for me the impulsion of belief as a Catholic. They are not always earnestly lived by, nor perfectly applied, but they infuse a moral and social code that I find congenial, ranging from concern for human life to regard for the quality of life. The most glaring of institutional flaws and the sorriest of institutional ministers do not shake my confidence and admiration for them. I might wish that bishops melted down their rings and their croziers; I might wish that the Church that preached the blessedness of the poor did not do so from sanctuaries of carved marble. Similarly I wish mightily for an improvement in the quality of the sermons intended to convey those values, and an end to sermons that shame those values. I think of one heard in Glenshaw, Pennsylvania, where we in the congregation were told to thank God we were white else we wouldn't be living in that allegedly wonderful parish . . . and of another heard in New Rochelle, New York, where a priest used the Sermon on the Mount to lecture the poor on their "arrogance." (Seems the priest had had a run-in a day or two before with an underpaid, "poor" attendant at a nearby mental hospital.) Sermons like those do a lot of damage to the faith of the hearers, and time was when they would have sent me screaming out the church door and joining a protest committee. But not in my present state of Catholicism. My anger subsides under renewed reflection that ours is a Church of humans. I stand willing to be convinced seven days of every week that the divinity of the Church is proved by the frailty of its members. Father Hans Küng once wrote, "It is possible to admire the Catholic Church without being a Catholic. And it is perhaps just as possible to be a Catholic without admiring it." I don't know that I'd go that far. I admire the Church warts and all, and I find it possible to be embarrassed by some who represent the Church without the foundations of my Catholicism being shaken. Resignation, or maturity? Or a combination of the two? I don't know that I can say exactly.

It may be that the Church itself is more mature and more sensitized as a result of Vatican II.

In any case, today I am happy to say that the low points as a Catholic are less frequent for me than they used to be. I can still get annoyed by the leadership's political involvements and the zealousness that it brings to issues of wider public concern than the denominational, including abortion and aid to parochial schools. At the same time, I would rather be a member of a Church whose excesses were on the side of life and the improved human condition than of a Church with no excesses at all and hardly anything to distinguish it from a kind of democratic humanism. That's another reason for my being Catholic.

The values I cherish in Catholicism were neatly summarized some time ago in a commentary to the New York *Times* by Archbishop Joseph L. Bernardin, former president of the National Conference of Catholic Bishops, when he spoke of "family values, a healthy and integrated acceptance of sexuality, stability in marital relations, a sense of obligation toward other persons, and willingness to accept the consequences of one's actions." Archbishop Bernardin was commenting in the context of abortion and teen-age pregnancies, and though he may have claimed more for Catholic tolerance and understanding in the area of human sexuality than the record would legitimately allow, he did sum up a value system that embraced much more than abortion and pregnancy positions, and that extended to social and behavioral issues generally. These values may not infuse modern America the way they once did, but they are the values that went into the building of the country, and of Western civilization itself, and they do make a society stable and responsible. I might not join those bishops who would impose them on the larger American society—the pluralistic society must be allowed its pluralism—but I do want them for me and my family.

Whether or not I apply them as directly in my life as I should, I want to see fostered those gospel values that sent a Dorothy Day to a life's work in the Bowery; that sent a Mother Teresa to a life of dedication and service among India's poorest; that sent a Daniel Berrigan to the streets in witness to peace and justice, and a Philip Berrigan and Elizabeth McAllister to jail for demonstrating against the madness of nuclear-weapons proliferation. I want to see fostered those gospel values that go into the making of the good parent, the faithful spouse, the loyal huband, the loving sons and daughters—those values that bring couples closer together, and to God, when times are toughest—those values that prompt young people to heroic service on behalf of others, in the Peace Corps, in Vista, in Catholic Charities, in the Indian missions, in volunteer programs of multiple kinds. The Catholic Church does not have a corner on these values; you don't have to be a believer, even, to bring these values into your life, much less be a Catholic. I merely maintain that in my case it helps—and reassures. For as Catholicism promotes and encourages these values, I get the added consolation of knowing that I belong to a Church that is relevant to the world around it. And committed to its welfare.

I am happy in my Church, although I would be less than honest if I did not confess that I am unnerved at times by the erosion that is taking place within it. It is constantly reassuring to me that so many persons whose intelligence and integrity I highly respect are continuing as Catholics. On the other hand, the departure of so many others of intelligence and integrity, most of whom I respect no less, does give me pause at times about my own instinct to remain so settled and contented a Catholic. Likewise, I would be less than honest if I did not confess that sometimes I get the glum feeling of being on a sinking ship, what with Catholic colleges and universities going broke, parochial schools closing down, Catholic hospitals slipping from religious control to ownership by nonsectarian, public boards. Even the liturgy that I love so much has gone to pot, and with it so much of that precious element that we call Catholic community. (How could it have been that those who labored so long and so heroically for a renewed and purified Mass could have been so totally unprepared to make good on what they prepared us for?)

Maybe my attitude is too passive, too resigned, too unquestioning, too anything. But I stick as Catholic and will continue to because Catholicism is my heritage and my hope. I'll let the cranks condemn the Church because it is not the Church of their day-to-day devising or needs. I'll let the cynics have their libelous little jokes about the post-Vatican II Church being hardly different from the pre-Vatican II Church, only the preservation of the old order by the making of modern noises, or only the rearranging of the same old furniture. I'll stick, because the post-Vatican II Church is a better Church; because it is more open, more compassionate, indeed more pluralistic, a place where a thousand flowers can of course grow. I'll stick because, deep down, I am convinced that the strength and verve of the Church will return; erosion and recovery are the history of Catholicism. And I'll stick because I am convinced that community will return, and very probably by way of the presently deficient new liturgy. That new liturgy has a future, I am sure—although Catholics generally must first become educated to the activist role that this liturgy imposes on them. Leave aside for now the abominable translation that weighs the new liturgy down; somewhere off in the future there is a Ronald Knox or some King-James scholars to straighten out the language of the Mass and make it inspirational. And beautiful. Focus instead on the new liturgy concept. It *does* have potential for the forging of community and the uplifting of souls, much as the Latin Mass did in the old days. But it will take work, and education, and time.

You experience the potential of the new liturgy on occasion, and it makes you so much the sadder for the routine of the usual Sunday morning. I experienced it twice within the year: at the eightieth-birthday Mass of Celebration for Dorothy Day at St. Joseph's Church in Greenwich Village, and at a nephew's wedding Mass at Assumption College in Worcester, Massachusetts. At Dorothy Day's Mass it was despite being cold and wet, chilled to the bone after sharing a disintegrating umbrella in a driving rainstorm with Frank Sheed, walking from a subway station three blocks away. At my nephew's nuptials, it was despite being dog-tired after a long and taxing drive from New York. Not only were spirits uplifted by these liturgies, but they soared—and eyes were opened at last to the inspiration that is possible in the new Mass. People sang lustily; they rejoiced; they shed the old Catholic inhibitions that tend to make Catholics at worship almost as telephone poles (Father H. A. Reinhold's observation). They embraced, they hugged, they kissed at the exchange of greetings. They loved one another, as the Scripture said they should. It was beautiful. You felt the Spirit in the pews around you, and you sensed that whatever produced this had to be of the right formula. The Latin Mass properly celebrated and participated in produced something of the same effect, often. But this was the new liturgy. One had a feeling of seeing the future, and seeing it work. One had a sense of the Church being back on track.

Unfortunately, special occasion, kin, and comradeship are not built into the new liturgy. They are not there in the mere coming together of people who share something in common. But they are there potentially all the time by being there part of the time, and that is what is more important. It may take a generation or more to develop the new liturgy; the Latin Mass, I am sure, wasn't made in a day. There is no reason to expect the new liturgy virtually overnight to be all that the liturgical visionaries (in the best of understandings) promised it would be. But the day will come. Tomorrow will be better for the grandchildren.

In the meantime, the broad challenge for many Catholics will be to be patient, and to hang tight, if only as cultural Catholics. Cultural Catholicism is a much disparaged concept at the moment, but being a cultural Catholic is not the indifferent or negative thing that many would make it. Many liberals tend to look down on cultural Catholicism as a Catholicism of convenience, a lingering phase for those too timid about making the clean, definitive break with their past. Conservatives, on the other hand, demean the concept as trite and pseudo-religious. "Baptized pagans," some conservatives label cultural Catholics. In a sense, the criticism on both sides has a validity. Yet being a cultural Catholic is one way of keeping in touch with one's roots, and not a bad way at that. It is no small thing to be a part of the heritage of Michelangelo and Meštrović, of Mozart and Ginastera, of Dante and Hopkins, of Francis of Assisi and Foucauld, of Elizabeth of Hungary and Elizabeth Seton, of Louise de Marillac and Dorothy Day, of Pasteur and Mendel, of Bernard of Clairvaux and Thomas Merton. Come to think of it, I could stay Catholic on the heritage alone of these people.

There were—are in the cases of any still living—no rigid orthodoxies in the religious attitudes of those Catholics, and little of the formalisms that some would make the yardstick of faith in discounting the cultural-Catholic idea. I refer, among others, to Monsignor Philippe Delhaye of the Vatican-based International Theology Commission, who would refuse the Church's blessing on the marriages of those who ostensibly never really "professed or lived their faith" and who want a Church wedding "to please their parents, or for some other worldly reason." Now of course Christian marriage is more than a social occasion or rite; it's also more than an ecclesiastical device to ease parental distress on a problem point in life. A truly Christian marriage presupposes a bond with the Christ of history. But a flintlike rigidness about who qualifies for the Church's blessing is a rejection of sorts of an implicit faith in those less orthodox Catholics who may still be feeling their way in life and belief. There have to be rules, to be sure. But they should not be of the kind that jams the doors of the future where these individuals are concerned.

It is important, therefore, that some middle ground be found that both protects the Church's theological and liturgical integrity and keeps the doors open to the increasingly large number of irregular Catholics. Saying it another way, the Church should not be quick about those it reads off the rolls, and it should be especially lenient toward young people who are living in unique times so far as freedom of conscience and independence of spirit are concerned—not all of which is sniffed from the air, be it said. Pope Pius XII back in 1945 preached of "the clear and incontrovertible dictates of conscience," and Vatican II, of course, repeatedly held in honor the laws of individual and social living written in the hearts of men. Today's Church should do no less in terms of the first full generations of Catholics born to this tradition.

Prelates like Philadelphia's Cardinal Krol like to say that the unorthodox of today will be the orthodox of tomorrow, that careless young believers will steady once their roots sink into marriage and they begin to have families of their own. This may be so much wishful thinking, but the idea doesn't even have a chance if young Catholics are alienated now on issues important to them in their seemingly marginal Catholicism. That is why the fostering of cultural Catholicism is vital, and why flexibility is necessary. A Church bound to the book of rules is not the Church by which anyone of the new generation is likely to regularize his or her life. In my stubbornness, I probably wouldn't either, if my situation were theirs.

All I'm saying is that if a dogmatic punctiliousness is presently impossible where large numbers of Catholics are involved, then better a cultural (and social) connection than no connection at all. Granted that the motives of some cultural Catholics may at times be suspect, that they may be calculating and insincere; and granted that there is always the possibility of the Church being "used." But better to leave the judgment on this to loftier authority. God, I expect, will be more convivial than the rule makers and interpreters.

In this context, the approach adopted by the bishops of the United States at their May 1978 meeting in Chicago is quite commendable. Estimating that 26 per cent of Catholics over eighteen years of age were essentially "churchless," and that the figure climbed to 40 per cent among those between eighteen and thirty, the bishops announced plans for a program of evangelization that will emphasize sharing rather than regimentation. "We used to say, 'We will make a Catholic out of you,'" said Archbishop Francis T. Hurley of Anchorage, Alaska, chairman of the evangelization committee. "But that was in the thirties and forties. Now we say, 'We have something to share with you.'"

This is the Church one loves, a Church of solicitousness and affection, a Church that ultimately will be best understood. A friend of mine read Archbishop Hurley's words and remarked, "Where the hell's the Church I rebelled against? It doesn't exist any more. My revolution is silly." Indeed it is. The "ogre" Church of yesterday has been replaced by the very Church that the rebellious of yesterday demanded. It's been replaced too by a concerned Church that those who faulted it for its detachment can be enthusiastic about. That's the discovery which awaits those who take the careful relook. Heaven forbid that when they do, they see a Church in the throes of a reactionaryism based on some ill-conceived opinion about "baptized pagans."

The intriguing point, by way of summation, is that the Church can be the tolerant Mother, can be true to itself dogmatically, can accommodate cultural Catholics and other types (many, at least), and it can still force upon each and all what most account to be the central questions of existence:

Who am I? What am I? Why am I here? What more is there to the life I call my own?

Speaking for myself, I am a Catholic because of the answers that the Church helps me furnish to those questions: I am a creature created in God's image, with an immortal soul and an eternal destiny, and with an attendant obligation to do something of God's work on this earth. I believe I can do this work best within and through the Church of God the Son, the Church of the Saints, the Church of the molders of Western civilization. I feel I can do it best within a Church that sings of joy and holds out the promise of eternal reward, a Church that is triumphant (sometimes exasperatingly so), but at the same time a Church that never lets me forget that God is forever to be found where human suffering is the most pronounced: in family crises, in sickness, in the ghetto, in prison, on the battlefield, at the poor farm, along the soup line.

There is an etching that appears periodically in *The Catholic Worker* which depicts Christ huddled anonymously in a queue of depressed and deprived persons. The etching is the art of the noted Fritz Eichenberg. Paradox or not, that etching by one who is not a Catholic sums up the essence of my own Catholicism.

When I get to the bottom line, I find I am a Catholic because the Catholic Church helps me discover Christ in the most unlikely places . . . and among the most unlikely of God's creatures.

WHY I REMAIN A CATHOLIC

Andrew Greeley

One of the most articulate American Catholic spokesmen of our times, Andrew Greeley is a native Chicagoan and received his S.T.B. and S.T.L. from St. Mary's Seminary, Mundelein, Illinois, and his doctorate in sociology from the University of Chicago. He was program director for the National Opinion Research Center of the University of Chicago in 1968–70 and became director of the Center for the Study of American Pluralism in 1971. He has written articles for scores of magazines—among them the New York *Times Magazine*, *The Critic*, *The Christian Century*, and *U. S. Catholic* —and lectures all over the United States. He is the author of more than forty books, which have had an enormous impact on the American Catholic scene, notably his sociological reports *The Education of Catholic Americans*, *American Priests*, and *Catholic Schools in a Declining Church*. Among his more recent books are *The Jesus Myth*, *An Ugly Little Secret*, and *Everything You Wanted to Know About the Church but Were Too Pious to Ask*. He also writes two syndicated columns, one for the Catholic press and one that appears in secular newspapers throughout the country.

When I was first asked to write this article, I must confess to being taken somewhat aback. "Why was I impelled to remain a Catholic?" I wasn't impelled at all. I am a Catholic because I want to be a Catholic. To be asked, "Why do you stay in the Church?" is like being asked why stay in the priesthood? Why leave?

Or as someone remarked, "Stay and bother them!"

Whatever other problems there have been in my life, I have not experienced a crisis of faith or of religious affiliation or of vocation. I'm sorry about that. Perhaps, not having experienced them, I may not have the proper sympathy for those that do; but in any case, the reader should be aware that this essay is not an account of a spiritual odyssey. (I'm not saying that I haven't had my spiritual odysseys, but to reveal them at the present time would not be to address myself to the assigned question.)

I must also note that the available research evidence indicates that a so-called "crisis of faith" (or of religious affiliation or of vocation) can be heavily influenced by unperceived forces which are scarcely religious. Thus, in his brilliant book *View from the Border* social psychologist John Kotre demonstrated how much one's perceptions of the Church are influenced by the tension and conflict in one's family. "Leaving the Church" is often an unconscious protest against one's parents. What seems to be religious conflict is in fact unresolved family conflict. Anyone who has done parish work has witnessed the phenomenon many times of a person who is convinced that his departure from the Church or from Christianity is a matter of pure intellect when in fact it is merely a way of punishing parents. God becomes a surrogate father, the Church a surrogate mother; by rejecting God and Church one nicely disposes of one's parents.

There is a substantial research literature in addition to Kotre's seminal work which supports that hypothesis—most notably *Religious Dropouts* by David Caplowitz; *Faith of Our Fathers*, a Ph.D. dissertation by William McCready; and a chapter on "religious disidentification" in my own *Crisis in the Churches*. Anyone who is attempting to analyze his relationship with his own religious tradition is simply kidding himself if he does not carefully and objectively consider the impact of his childhood family conflicts on his so-called religious crisis. As Kotre wisely pointed out, the Church is a phenomenon which emits many different cues. Whether you choose to focus on the cues that enable you to stay in it or those that excuse you for leaving it is not a function of the nature of the Church so much as a function of the personality conflicts you bring to your confrontation with the Church.

I therefore have not experienced any crisis of religious affiliation, and I have a professional skepticism about some of the tales of such crises. (This is not to say that I believe the crises are not real or painful but only that all the dynamics at work are not always faced honestly.)

I can conceive four different sets of reasons for leaving the Church: institutional, doctrinal, imaginative, and religious. The institutional reasons—which are, it seems to me, the most often cited—are poor, indeed ridiculous, reasons for disengaging from Catholicism. Doctrinal reasons are somewhat better but still not very good. Objections to the "Catholic imagination" are, however, excellent reasons for leaving the Church—but only derivatively. The best reasons for leaving Catholicism are religious. They are the only ones that make any sense at all; they are also the ones most infrequently mentioned as grounds for disengaging from the Church.

By considering these four sets of reasons for not being a Catholic, I will articulate my reasons for staying in the Church, reasons which have been implicit, I suppose, in my life all along. I shall attempt to make this discussion of the reasons for staying or leaving as personal as possible.

I have three major disillusionments in my relationship with the institutional Church—the failure of Paul VI to carry out the spirit of the Vatican Council, the destruction of my own archdiocese by a bizarre (not to use more accurate and potentially libelous adjectives) archbishop, my own ostracization from the priesthood.

First of all, the Second Vatican Council was one of the great religious events in human history, as was the reign of Pope John XXIII, one of the truly extraordinary wonders of grace in the whole two-millennium existence of Catholic Christianity. The Second Vatican Council was a time of "kairos," a time of extraordinary opportunity which has been wasted for the most part. Doubtless in the wild euphoria after the first session of the Council there were unrealistic hopes and naive expectation. Nonetheless, Pope John managed to capture the attention of the world and captivate the energies and enthusiasms of Christians in a way few pontiffs have. Extraordinarily powerful energies were released, particularly at the first session of the Council. Positive dynamics swirled toward the Church which could have led to extraordinary growth. The Church was finally saying the right things in the right way at the right time to a world desperately looking for religious leadership. The pope and the Council seemed to symbolize all the perennial strength and the ever-present newness of the Catholic Christian tradition.

In the United States in particular the Church, in the final stages of the immigrant era, was strong, vigorous, confident, though the American bishops at the Council only dimly perceived it. The Council was, nonetheless, a fairly American event. Many of the ideas which became universal Catholic teaching at the Council had been anticipated by the great Americanists of the late nineteenth century. Confidence, openness, ecumenism, pragmatism, decentralization, pluralism, which were enthusiastically endorsed by an overwhelming majority of the Council fathers, were preached seventy-five years previously by such giants of American Catholicism as Ireland, Gibbons, Keene, Spaulding. Immigrant Catholicism could have easily and almost painlessly shifted into the ecumenical age with relatively few losses and major gains. I am arguing, it will be obvious to the reader, that the postconciliar disillusionment was neither necessary or inevitable, that much of the promise of Vatican II could have been achieved, at least in the United States, with relative ease, that the present crisis of decline in American Catholicism was not created by any inevitable, historical mechanism such as "secularization" but was rather the result of unconscionably bad decisions made first in Rome and then, imitating Rome, by the leadership of the American Church.

The story of postconciliar disillusionment, particularly among priests and religious of my generation, has been told so often as to become a cliché. Cliché or not, it is still true.

One often hears it said that Pope Paul will be judged more kindly by history than he has been by his contemporaries. I do not believe this for a minute. History, it seems to me, will be very harsh indeed on Paul VI. He will be seen as one who came in the fullness of time and understood nothing of that time. It will charge that he was not, as some of his admirers have argued, a prisoner of the curial reaction to the Council but the leader of that reaction—however unintentionally and however good his motives. History will say that Paul VI had a faulty sociological, theological, and historical understanding of the nature of the power of the papacy, that to protect what he perceived to be the papal powers he shamelessly abused them, and instead of protecting and strengthening the tradition of the papacy—as was surely his intent—he in fact dangerously weakened those powers. In particular, I am convinced that history will judge that the encyclical letter *Humanae Vitae*, however noble its motivation, was one of the worst mistakes of the Christian era—not merely because of misunderstood human sexuality and misunderstood natural law, not even because its theology of the papacy was woefully mistaken, but most of all because it destroyed the positive élan which Paul's predecessor unleashed with the convening of the Council.

The impact of Paul's reign and the birth-control encyclical on the American Church is plain for all to see. There is a kind of pseudo-sophisticated historicism to be found among the Catholic elites in this country which argues that deterioration after the Council was inevitable, though the birth-control encyclical may have accelerated the rate of deterioration. But such a reading of the history of the past fifteen years is wrong, the sort of mindless superficiality one has come to expect from the half-educated Catholic elites. My colleagues William McCready and Kathleen McCourt and I demonstrated with more evidence than one can ordinarily expect in such inquiries that the Vatican Council was an immense success for American Catholicism. It unleashed extraordinarily rich and positive dynamics, and the devastation we witnessed in the American Church was the result of the Pauline Reaction and in particular the birth-control encyclical. It is a misunderstanding of the nature of the human condition to think that everything that has happened had to happen. In fact, the postconciliar reaction with such devastating effect did not have to happen at all.

The needless destruction was nowhere worse than in the archdiocese of Chicago. Much of what was best in the final stages of immigrant Catholicism—marriage education, the specialized Catholic Action movements, the new catechetics, liturgical revival, apostolate to the Spanish-speaking, community action—had originated and prospered in Chicago under the leadership of Cardinals Stritch and Meyer. Of all the large archdioceses in the country Chicago was the one best equipped to respond to the opportunities presented by the Vatican Council renewal. All of those experiments have vanished, and the institutional Church—schools, cemeteries, charities, seminaries—have begun to erode, perhaps beyond the point of no return. I have heard prominent Catholic prelates all over the United States and in Rome admit that the Cody appointment was a disastrous mistake, concede that our archbishop ought to be replaced, and then shrug their shoulders hopelessly. In other words, it is better that the whole people should suffer than that one cardinal of proven incompetency be replaced.

My third disillusionment came when I discovered that the mythology of the great "priestly fraternity," which I had learned in the seminary and which I deeply believed, was a falsehood. Priests are very much like peasants; that is, they live in a society of very limited resources and bitterly resent any one of their number who seems to be getting a disproportionate share. Apparently they think that if anyone gets more than they do, it is somehow or other at their expense. A substantial number of my fellow priests find that I have become an inkblot into which they can project their own discontent and frustrations. The resentment is not aimed at what I write, because few priests read it, or my person, because relatively few know me; it is rather that I write and that I am. It is reinforced by such clerically oriented journals as *The National Catholic Reporter*, *Commonweal*, and *America*. Objective scholarship, one discovers, has no market value unless it corresponds to the inkblot generated by clerical envy.

Naively, I guess, I had expected support of my fellow priests when I began to write. Instead, I encountered bitter resentment at the modest recognition that my work earned, a resentment still so strong that it would, if it could, blot out my work, a resentment which when it cannot hurt me directly turns to the persecution of members of my family. People tell me that I shouldn't be surprised by clerical resentment. Given the ideals, if not the reality, of the priesthood, I think I should; and in any event I am surprised and profoundly disillusioned.

I speak of these three disillusionments precisely because I wish to convince the reader that I am not unacquainted with surprise, disappointment, and pain from the institutional Church. My disappointments may not be your disappointments, but it is futile to argue about whose disillusionments have been the more severe, whom the institutional Church has betrayed the most. I merely want to demonstrate that I understand personally the argument against Catholicism that can be based on personal disillusionment—perhaps the most frequently heard excuse for disengaging from Catholic Christianity.

The argument is worthless.

One may be properly outraged by the betrayal of the ideals of Christianity by the institutional Church; one must, if one is a committed Christian, struggle for the reform of the institutional Church: *Ecclesia semper reformanda*. A church which could not disillusion, which could not cause personal pain and suffering, would be a church made up of archangels. Any ecclesial body composed of human beings will certainly disillusion. Search for the perfect church if you will; when you find it, join it, and realize that on that day it becomes something less than perfect.

The reader can make up his own litany of injuries the Catholic Church has done to him. I do not care how horrendous that litany may be, it does not provide a valid excuse for disengaging from the Catholic Christian heritage. Indeed, it is irrelevant. I attempt no justification and offer no excuse for what the Church may have done to you; I simply assert that the failures of Christians and the failures of Christian leadership have nothing to do with the validity of the Catholic Christian heritage. If you use those failures as an excuse for not facing the essential religious demands of the Catholic Christian heritage, you are engaged in an intellectually dishonest copout. The question is not whether the Catholic leadership is enlightened but whether Catholicism is true. A whole College of Cardinals filled with psychopathic tyrants provides no answer one way or another to that question.

The second set of reasons for decamping from Catholicism has to do with objections to specific "doctrines" of Catholic Christianity—birth control, papal infallibility, transubstantiation, the existence of angels, the divinity of Jesus. It is curious that even when the most sophisticated people advance such "doctrines" as reasons for no longer identifying with the Catholic heritage, they insist on interpreting those doctrines in the most fundamentalistic way possible and adamantly refuse to listen to serious discussion about the sense or the meaning of the doctrine. It is as though the Catholic heritage is a checklist of doctrinal propositions, each one of which must be accepted in its literal wording if one wishes to remain inside the tradition. Just as those who plead institutional disillusionment as an excuse for leaving the heritage stack the deck against Catholicism, so too those who depart on doctrinal grounds. Both define the game in such a way that the tradition doesn't stand a chance. The former will not accept a church composed of imperfect and limited human beings; the latter will not consider the possibility of a heritage in which there are only a few things one has to believe but those very strongly.

Let us take a doctrine which seems to create problems for many young people—the divinity of Jesus. Many young people with sixteen years of Catholic education insist on interpreting this doctrine in Docetist terms (Jesus only appeared to be a man) or Monophysite terms (Jesus is only God and not really man at all). This essay is scarcely the place to develop a restatement of Catholicism's Christology. There is evidence that most of those who find problems in the "divinity" of Jesus do not understand the issue. For those interested in pursuing the subject, I would recommend *The Foundations of Faith* by Karl Rahner, the distinguished German theologian and member of the Papal Theological Commission.

The divinity of Jesus, then, may well be a religious problem, but one ought to conclude that it is only after making a serious attempt to understand the implications of the doctrine. To reject it before finding out what it means is intellectually dishonest, a copout in facing the religious challenge of Christianity, as is the escape justified by the human imperfections of the Church. To go forth from the Catholic heritage because of what a nun said in fifth grade or what a priest told me in high school about papal infallibility or birth control is not only to misunderstand the challenge of Catholic Christianity but to inexcusably avoid the challenge. I'm sorry, but when I hear people raise those kinds of issues I find myself beginning to wonder what sort of childhood conflicts they're trying to work out.

A much better set of reasons for disaffiliating with Catholic Christianity can be found in what might loosely be called the "Catholic anthropology"—the Catholic view of the nature of human nature and the nature of human society, a view, which as David Tracy has pointed out, is a product of the "Catholic imagination." This perspective is not so much a matter of Catholic doctrine as a way of looking at things which seems to develop in those whose thinking and imagination is shaped by the Catholic heritage. Briefly, this "Catholic anthropology" can be summarized as follows:

1. As Camus put it in the conclusion of his novel *The Plague*, "There is more to be admired in human nature than to be contemned." Human nature, on balance, is more good than bad.

2. Human society is not made up of isolated, atomized individuals, struggling for their freedom against the crushing leviathan of society. Rather, human individuals exist as members of dense, organic, and overlapping networks which exist not to curtail their freedom (at least not necessarily) but to enhance and promote the development of authentic personhood.

3. Hence, the Catholic imagination is convinced of the importance of local community, neighborhood, traditional, and historical ties, the "rootedness" of the human condition. It accepts as neither possible nor desirable the goal of temporary, "transient," "mobile" humankind which can be molded, modeled, and reshaped to fit the master plans of either capitalist or socialist bureaucracy.

4. "Catholic anthropology" tends to favor, therefore, decentralization, the "principle of subsidiarity," grass-roots control, and informal, casual, piecemeal reform instead of a priori-blueprint approaches to social action. It believes in organic, evolutionary growth rather than dramatic, revolutionary, sweeping-the-slate-clean-to-start-all-over-again upheaval.

David Tracy, in his *The Analogical Imagination*, explains

the theological roots of this "Catholic anthropology." In my own *No Bigger Than Necessary* I advance sociological data to show that Catholics do behave in ways that one would predict from such a perspective. In the present essay it suffices to say that much of the difference between Catholics and Protestant Christians and non-Christians in the ordinary world of daily life can be traced to this "analogical anthropology." The differences, let us say, between *America* and *The Christian Century* are stylistic far more than doctrinal in this ecumenical age. *America* will never be quite as guilt-ridden as *The Christian Century*, even in its most frantic liberation-theology moments, nor as pessimistic and frantically anxious about the human condition, nor as dramatic in its clarion calls for "total renewal." (Once *Christian Century* editor James Wall's friend Jimmy Carter was elected President of the United States, the magazine began to see a good deal more complexity in politics than it had witnessed previously.) These stylistic differences flow from implicitly different anthropologies, which are usually not articulated but which have profound impact on human behavior and cause immense confusion when Catholic Christians interact in cooperative efforts—whether in marriage or world conferences—with other Christians or non-Christians.

The Catholic view of the nature of human nature is far too pessimistic by the standards of liberals and socialists who think that if one remakes the structures of society one can rather quickly mold an entirely new kind of human nature. But it is far too optimistic, at least far too hopeful, for Reformation pessimism about human sinfulness. (Reinhold Niebuhr, that quintessential Protestant anthropologist, dismisses the Catholic theory of the nature of human nature as "semi-Pelagianism"—an optimistic heresy!)

Similarly, the Catholic view of the nature of human society is "reactionary" by the standards of liberal humanism which sees the individual as almost totally autonomous, able to guide himself on a universalistic rational path, free from bonds of particularism and tradition. On the other hand, the Catholic imagination is far more at ease with technology in the rational use for human good of the resources of this world than is the new frugal, puritanical environmentalism of the ecological movement. Catholic Christians, in other words, because of their religious perspective tend to take certain positions on humankind and human society which are unacceptable to those who hold other perspectives or ideologies. If you really think that human nature is more bad than good, that particularity, localism, and tradition can be eliminated from the human condition, if you believe in a malleable human nature that can be remade by changing the structures of society, or if you believe in centralized, bureaucratically administered planning in an essentially homogeneous society instead of pluralistic messiness, then you will find yourself ill at ease with the Catholic heritage.

The differences in anthropological perspective, of course, are not rigid and sharp. I am speaking of propensities and tendencies rather than fixed positions. Some non-Catholics may be much more ardent "subsidiarists" than many Catholics, and some Catholics may be much more intolerant of pluralism than many non-Catholics. Still there are important differences in anthropological perspective, and these differences can be traced to fundamental theological diversity and also can be documented by basic behavioral differences in social circumstances. To tell you the truth, I don't know of anyone who has left the Church because he cannot accept the principle of subsidiarity (nothing should be done by a higher or larger institution that can be done by a lower or smaller one). But it would make much better sense, I think, to depart from Catholic Christianity because of the principle of subsidiarity (which one might view as either shockingly revolutionary or shockingly old fashioned) than to leave it because of the birth-control encyclical or the behavior of Catholic bishops.

As it happens, I think that the principle of subsidiarity is correct and that the Catholic view of the nature of humankind and human society is the most fruitful and productive one with which to approach life in this world. When it comes to the question of why I am still a Catholic, one very solid answer would be that I am committed to the Catholic imagination, I buy the Catholic anthropology, I accept enthusiastically the Catholic social ethic.

In the current discussion of Catholicism one hears very little of the merits of its anthropology. I suspect that is because most of those of us who were raised under the impact of what Father Tracy calls "the analogical imagination" are much like M. Jourdain, in Molière's play *Le Bourgeois Gentilhomme*, who discovered to his astonishment that he was speaking prose. We have taken the Catholic anthropology for granted and it rarely occurs to us that others totally disagree with it, do not find it as reasonable, as plausible, and as self-evident as we do. Indeed, we can leave Catholicism and carry its anthropological perspective along with us with only the faintest realization that this perspective with which we continue to live is linked, at least insofar as its origins within our personality are concerned, to the Catholic religious heritage.

But there is only one good reason for separating oneself from the Catholic tradition. Catholicism is a religion; that is to say, it purports to give Final Meaning and Ultimate Interpretation to the nature and purposes of human life and of the cosmos in which humans find themselves. Hence, if Catholicism is to be authentically rejected, it must be rejected for *religious* reasons. Its interpretation of the meaning of human existence must finally be judged deficient; all other reasons are inadequate.

The issue is not whether Christ is divine but what Christ came to reveal about God and hence about the purpose of human life; for our notions about "God" are shorthand symbols for what we believe our existence is all about. There are many different ways of summarizing the Catholic world view. Each is ultimately personal, and hence my summary will be personal. It is, nonetheless, an accurate, if obviously not totally adequate summary.

The final trouble with Christianity is that it is too good to be true. The God revealed fully in Jesus and anticipated in the Jewish Scriptures is a God of enormous love, a God who enters into intimate personal relationship with his creatures.

Creation is an act of love, an initiation of a love affair, a gracious gift, an attempt to seduce the creature into loving response to the gift that has been given. The cosmos is a love affair, life is a romance whose purpose is the giving and receiving of love. Christianity is a response to the basic human question—perhaps the only religious question that really matters—of whether we dare trust that hopefulness which, try as we might, we cannot erase from our personality. The Christian response to the human hopefulness suffers from defect, not excess; we are not too hopeful but rather not hopeful enough. We can push our hope out to the outer limits of imagination, we can dream the impossible dream, fantasize the impossible vision, and when imagination, dream, and fantasy end, that which God's love has prepared for us only begins. "Eye has not seen, nor ear heard, nor has it entered into the heart of man . . ."

Life, then, means hope and love. Life, as G. K. Chesterton has said, is too important to be anything but life. Good conquers evil (if only just barely), love triumphs over hate (though by a hairbreadth), and life is victorious over death (though only at the last moment). Our existence is a curious mixture of suffering and joy. Catholic Christianity is committed to the notion that the suffering will pass away and that the joy is revelation.

I must insist that this is not "mere poetry," though it is poetry. One can speak of ultimate things only in pictures, images, and symbols; indeed, one can talk about God only by telling stories. But the stories are not wild exaggerations of the reality; they are, rather, weak and inadequate underestimations of it. To say that the story of the universe is a love affair is not to exaggerate but to be pitifully inadequate.

I cannot "prove" that the Catholic Christian story is true; I can only assert my faith that it is. To say that I continue to be a Catholic Christian is to say that I believe in the truth, however inadequate, of the story of the improbable God who permitted himself to be seduced by his own creatures, who fell in love with the apparently useless and worthless humans he created. Believing the truth of this story and believing that it is the only thing that really matters in Catholic Christianity, I am forced to assert that disbelief in the story's truth is the only good reason for getting out of Catholic Christianity. If you don't believe that the metaphor "God is love" is an understatement of the purpose of the cosmos, then by all means get out. If you think it is true, stay. If you hesitate in between, at least try to understand that you can never be free of the temptation of the Catholic Christian tradition until you have made up your mind one way or another.

Is it necessary to be a "Catholic" to be committed to the truth of the Christian story? Obviously it is not, though I cannot overcome the temptation of quoting James Joyce's famous response when asked why, when he left behind his Irish Catholicism, he did not become a Protestant. "Good heavens, sir, I may have lost my faith; but I have not lost my mind!" This is a personal reaction, not one that I am in any way suggesting should be normative for others. I continue to be a *Catholic* Christian because, first of all, I was born and raised one and because it is within the boundaries of the Roman Church that the Good News of Jesus was first preached to me by family, teachers, parish clergy, and friends. It is within the structure of that Church—however tragically and sometimes hopelessly imperfect it seems to be—that I continue to draw my basic religious support, nurture, and vitality. Psychologically I could not be any other kind of Christian and would not want to be. It may not be much of a church just now, but it's the only one I have. I do not delude myself that I could find other and better churches to sustain my Christian commitment elsewhere.

I am also committed to the Catholic anthropology, which I mentioned previously in this essay. I am convinced that that anthropology flows throughout the Christian revelation and mediates between it and human life far more adequately than do non-Catholic Christian anthropologies. I also find the Catholic conviction that salvation is communal rather than individualistic far more attractive than the opposite Protestant ecclesiologies. Everything else that humans do is ineluctably social; so, too, must be our response to God's love.

Finally, without going into it in any great detail, it does seem to me that the Catholic heritage and tradition has by far the better of the argument about historical continuity with the Christian past. I am not disposed to argue with others on this point; I simply say that toward the bottom of my own personal reasons for remaining a *Catholic* Christian is the matter of historical continuity.*

By "Catholic heritage" I mean many different things, some essential, others less so. Devotion to Mary, reverence for the material world, the cult of patron saints and special blessings (largely forgotten, I fear, in the "new" Church), the sacramental system, the ceremonies of the Mass (far better in English, if you ask me), the recognition of the importance of strong leadership and decentralized control (however much these may be violated in practice), patronage of the arts, architecture, and music as representative of the Church's belief in the goodness of all things human, the great history of theologians from Ignatius of Antioch to David Tracy, and the missionaries from Paul through Patrick to the contemporary Maryknollers, the pageantry of our ceremonies (sometimes rigid, sometimes overdone, but still potentially very powerful), the clear and indisputable linkage with and respect for the past, confidence (at least some of the time) in the goodness of the created world and the capacity of human intelligence; the nuanced view of human nature, thinking it neither totally good nor totally bad but on the whole, as Camus said, more to be admired than contemned; the broad Thomistic synthesis that, as men like Bernard Lonergan and Karl Rahner have recently demonstrated, is still alive and well. In my own personal life it was the extraordinarily powerful influence of priest, religious, and laity in the two

* For the benefit of the heresy searchers of the Sacred Congregation for the Doctrine of the Faith, let me add that I am well aware there are many other reasons for being a *Catholic* Christian. By listing the ones that have the strongest personal appeal to me, I am not excluding the importance of others.

parishes in which I learned the most about Catholicism—St. Angela, the parish of my childhood, and Christ the King, the parish of my young priesthood. All these are part of the Catholic heritage. I see no reason for giving it up; I do not want to give it up. Oh, no, I'm not going to leave those things behind—indeed, they couldn't drive me away!

The Catholic Church remains for me what it always has been—the parish in which I grew up, the parish in which I worked for the first ten years as a priest, my Catholic friends and family who patiently and lovingly sustained me in my faith, the loose-knit band of brothers and sisters who are the extended "neighborhood" on those streets I walk. It's not much of a church, perhaps, but it's the only one I have, and I love it desperately.

Leave it? No way.

ETERNITY'S ABIDING PRESENCE

JAMES HITCHCOCK

Born in St. Louis, Missouri, James Hitchcock received his A.B. from St. Louis University and his M.A. and Ph.D. from Princeton. He taught at St. John's and Long Island Universities in New York and then went to St. Louis University, where he is now a professor of history. He is chairman of the board of the Catholic League for Civil and Religious Rights, chairman of the Catholic Liturgy Association, vice-president of the Fellowship of Catholic Scholars, and editor of the quarterly journal *Communio*. He is a member of Phi Beta Kappa, Alpha Sigma Nu, the Jesuit honor society, the Catholic Historical Association, the American Historical Association, and the American Society for Reformation Research. He has written for a wide variety of periodicals, among them the New York *Times Magazine*, *Commentary*, *Yale Review*, *The American Scholar*, and *The Christian Century*, and is the author of *The Decline and Fall of Catholic Radicalism* and *The Recovery of the Sacred*.

It is a measure of our times that, when a question like "Why am I a Catholic?" is asked, the answers that instinctively come to mind tend to be pragmatic ones—because being a Catholic helps me to find meaning in life or to express myself fully as a person, or because Catholicism helps to make a better world or alleviates the sufferings of those in need.

Such assertions, while not irrelevant, fall a good deal short of answering the question. Our unmetaphysical age (one might even say antimetaphysical age) seems not to want to address itself to the most obvious answer that can and must be given to such a question. "I am a Catholic because I believe Catholicism is true." Whatever validity other answers may have, they have none in and of themselves. They are meaningful only if the truth of Catholic teaching is first accepted.

I say that these common responses are a measure of our times because I think they show how deeply certain very un-Catholic modes of thinking have come to be almost unquestioningly accepted in the Church in a short period of time. Prior to the Second Vatican Council few Catholics would have doubted that an assertion of doctrinal truth was basic to the Church's claims; we were, if anything, perhaps ultrarationalistic, too much taken with argument and logical persuasion. However, the influence of Romanticism with its assertion that Christianity is beautiful, or liberal Protestantism with its conviction that it can be practically useful, has now seeped into our bones. We are awash in the therapeutic habit of mind which cares only about what a thing means "for me" and not what it is or may be in itself.

Having said this, I am somewhat embarrassed, since I am neither by profession nor by temperament a metaphysician. To the degree that I understand it, I would subscribe to Cardinal Newman's *Essay in Aid of a Grammar of Assent* as perhaps the best statement of a Christian (and ultimately Catholic) apologetic that I know of. I find classical Scholastic argumentation more or less convincing on a formal level, but ("for me") somewhat lacking in ultimate persuasion.

The question "Why am I a Catholic?" immediately confronts us with one of the classic paradoxes of Christianity, for which we have no answer. In the last analysis, if we take Christian doctrine seriously, we have to say that we do not know the answer to that question, for the answer lies in the realm of God's grace and His providence. As Catholics we do not believe in the classic formulation of the doctrine of predestination, yet it is also clear that tangible, comprehensible, human explanations of the presence of faith in certain lives take us only so far. Another of the dangers of our time is the tendency to think almost exclusively in human terms, as though we could instill faith in our children, for example, by creating the proper familial and educational environment. We have less of a sense than we used to have of how much we depend on God's dispositions of our requests and desires. That faith is a gift, and that we must pray for its reception and preservation is something we often now lose sight of.

At first glance the idea contained in Christ's awful admonition, "You have not chosen Me; I have chosen you," may seem self-serving and flattering to the ego of the one chosen, and certainly there has been no lack of Christians, throughout history, who have taken it as a guarantee of privilege and status. But the reverse is, of course, really true—the gift of faith is a humbling thing not only because of the awareness it brings of one's unworthiness but also because it cannot help but dawn on any normally sensitive person that it is, from a human standpoint, a gift bestowed almost arbitrarily. As recipients of this gift we are less like victors in a race than winners in a lottery, although God must indeed have His own purposes.

In the past fifteen years, one of the great periods of crisis in the Church's history, I have been struck over and over again at the number of people whose faith was, evidently, more intense, better informed, and more fruitful than mine, who nonetheless seemed to lose it, or give it up, or willingly exchange it for something inferior. I can find no particular personal merit in my own perseverance in faith; God makes use of whatever instruments He chooses.

There is much effort expended in our time trying to re-make Catholicism in such a way as to render it "relevant to modern man," or to alleviate the objections which certain modern men may have to it. I think this activity is misconceived on several grounds. It is, quite obviously, a strategic error—the history of modern Christianity shows rather conclusively that, while efforts to redefine belief may be meaningful to people who are already Christians and who are experiencing problems of faith, they do little to attract skeptics into the churches. On the contrary, they merely serve to confirm the skeptics in their conviction that Christianity is indeed outmoded and irrelevant, because believers themselves are willing to jettison so much of its historical baggage.

There is also fundamental objection to this modernizing process which arises from the nature of Catholicism itself and of its claims to truth. Catholicism is perhaps the boldest of all religions precisely in hazarding so much on those claims. It is not content to be accepted for its utility, or the beautiful poetry of its symbols, although there have always been people who have approached it primarily for such reasons. It rather insists that it stands or falls on its claims to teach truth, an assertion that in one sense renders it highly vulnerable in a skeptical age and that also suggests that attempts to relativize its doctrines are not acts of courage, as they are often presented, but flights to security. If the doctrines of the Church are true, then most of the practical objections made against it are essentially irrelevant; while, if they are not true, the Church has been party to a gigantic historical fraud and cannot and should not be rehabilitated by any "updating" process.

There is a Scholastic or metaphysical approach to Catholicism that establishes its essence from an examination of doctrinal statements made over the centuries. Such an approach is now often dismissed as dependent on modes of thinking which are no longer valid. Without entering into that particular controversy, it seems to me that one arrives at a very similar understanding of the Church by employing a purely historical (perhaps even phenomenological) method. Whatever else it is, the Catholic Church is a historical entity which has manifested a particular identity throughout history. Like all historical entities, it is what it is and it cannot be arbitrarily redefined as something else. Much contemporary talk about the Church, by very well-meaning people, suffers from the apparent delusion that it is possible to define that church merely as one would like it to be, without regard for what it really is and has been.

Looking at the Church both as a historian and as one who has lived within it for forty years, I see it as manifesting certain very obvious characteristics which cannot be ignored or wished away. Among the most important of these are: a conviction of the importance of dogma and of dogmatic formulations, hence of doctrinal orthodoxy; the irrepressible propensity to express its beliefs through ritual and symbol; a clearly defined and detailed moral code; an unwavering conviction that the meaning of time is found only in eternity; a strong respect for tradition; and a hierarchical structure. Whatever does not possess these characteristics, however good and desirable it may be in itself, cannot be called authentically Catholic.

Personally I find fideism—the idea that God's truth is so far above human reason that all we can do is humbly believe, however little such belief may correspond to our own rational perceptions—rather appealing. I think it also must be recognized that some kind of fideism has, throughout history, had a very powerful appeal to some very great minds and personalities, the sense that one must simply submit—the intellect, the will, the whole person—to the divine being. The characteristics of historical Catholicism which I have outlined above are things which do not appear to have inherent appeal or plausibility to many people in our own age. Words like dogma and hierarchy seem almost guaranteed to provoke negative reactions. I am tempted at this point to take a purely fideistic stance and to say that, precisely because they are uncongenial and even offensive, they must be taken all the more seriously, that ultimately what God requires of us is our submission.

However, I stop just short of saying this because, while submission is (historically considered) an essential element of all religion and one which contemporary Christianity tries to wish away, God is also love and He is truth. It is not blind obedience which He seeks from His people.

I am enough a child of my times to understand why some people are horrified at the very thought of a dogmatic, traditional, hierarchical institution like the Catholic Church. At the same time I have to say that for me these aspects of its existence have never been sources of great offense or anguish. Had I not been born a Catholic, or had my experiences within the Church been different, perhaps I would now feel differently. Once again such vagaries of history are somehow within the scope of God's mysterious providence. However, while insisting that one's personal feelings are ultimately not the appropriate standard of judgment concerning right and wrong, truth and falsehood, I also ask those who are severely offended by what the historical Catholic Church is and always has been to consider whether their experience is necessarily the only possible one.

Probably no feature of the Catholic Church arouses so much immediate antagonism as the idea of dogma and its accompanying idea of authority. To claim to be able to define truths with certitude, to pronounce that certain formulations are erroneous and even heretical, to insist that there exists an authority which is able to distinguish truth from falsehood, is to invite total rejection from those segments of the world which consider themselves modern, even within the Church itself.

I have nothing new to say on this subject. If the idea of dogma, and its accompaniments, is to be declared false, this must surely be done on some grounds more profound than the tastes of a particular age. The circumstances of dogma's rejection themselves point towards its importance. Leaving aside the claim of divine authority (without which, of course, it is ultimately meaningless), dogma is surely important precisely because it protects us from the unrestrained enthusiasm of a particular historical period. Humanly speaking, dogma is the means by which a community like the Church endeavors to salvage as much as possible from the wreck of each particular historical epoch, the almost fanatical drive which each epoch manifests to remold all of reality to suit its own specifications. In proclaiming dogmas, the Church is telling us something very hopeful—that there is a truth which we can know despite the inevitable limitations of our own perceptions, and that our knowledge of this truth can withstand shifting historical patterns. We are not mere prisoners of history but have the freedom of those to whom the truth has been revealed.

The word dogma almost inevitably conjures up negative reactions in our time, but it is worth recalling that not so many years ago the fact of Catholic dogma was for many people an integral part of the Church's appeal and credibility. This was especially true of so many of the great intellectual converts of the past century and a half, beginning with John Henry Newman. The radical reversal of mood among the intellectual classes which has led to dogma's present discredit should be treated as precisely that—a mood, a possibly quite temporary shift in feeling that may well reverse itself once again. (Political dogmatism is never out of fashion for very long in intellectual circles.)

If I were given a word-association test with regard to the Catholic Church, I think the word which would leap most immediately to mind would be "richness." Instinctively I sense Catholicism as representative of a far more complex, profound, and variegated kind of reality than any other creed with which I am familiar. If the word dogma calls forth hostility from the modern mind, the word heresy is almost guaranteed to summon benign feelings. A heretic, after all, is someone who insists on uttering inconvenient truths which those in authority would rather not hear. He dares to assert the sacredness of individual conscience in the face of repressive authority. How can modern man not admire and respect such a person?

We forget, however, that a heretic, from the Church's standpoint, means someone who picks and chooses, who deliberately takes the part for the whole. I have never found heresy attractive (although particular heresies may have attractive things about them), because it means the impoverishment of richness, the emptying of the depths, the rendering simplistic of what is and ought to be complex. So also it seems to me that there cannot be anything of grandeur about heresy, although individual heretics may be brave and sincere people, because heresy always stubbornly tends toward reductionism, energizes its sometimes fanatic zeal on behalf of a narrowed and impoverished view of reality. Instinctively I feel that what is individualistic, what pits private judgment against communal wisdom, is likely to be destructive and corrosive of truth and goodness.

In a sense I think that contemporary heresies, understood as either attacks on or radical modifications of established Catholic dogma, are among the least interesting in the entire history of the Church. The classic doctrinal controversies, such as those early ones surrounding the nature and identity of Christ, were courageous ventures onto uncharted waters by bold and powerful minds. What passes for an equivalent boldness today often seems to emanate from personal pique of some kind, which is quickly rewarded by media adulation, and it is the familiar attempt to take the rich stew which is historical Catholicism and reduce it to a supposedly more palatable thin soup.

This reduction directly relates to another of the basic notes of Catholicism which I have identified—its preoccupation with eternity. It seems to me that, if the pressures to "renew" the Church in our time can be reduced to a single idea, it is the wish to foreswear eternity, not to permit it to intrude into the comfortable confines of mundane life, to "explain" the doctrines and symbols of the Church in purely human and temporal ways. In Dwight McDonald's phrase from a slightly different context, it aims "to turn down the voltage so as not to blow a fuse." It caters to the apparent desire of many people for a comfortable, even a cozy, kind of religion.

In insisting on the reality of eternity, and not only its reality but also its central significance to human life, the Church is taking an enormous gamble. I suspect that even in the staunchest "ages of faith" many people have often felt themselves so deeply immersed in the undeniable denseness of daily life that the notion of eternal life seemed to them extremely remote and improbable. We cannot evade the central necessity of faith—ultimately our conviction that we have an eternal destiny rests not on whatever "intimations of immortality" we may experience but on the promises of Christ, of which our experiences may not necessarily give much of an inkling.

In speaking about the reality of eternity I do not merely refer to personal immortality, to life after death, but also to the idea that there exists a transcendent eternal realm within which our time-bound existences are, as it were, a kind of parenthesis. There are the staggering implications of the doctrine of the Trinity—the eternal generation of the Word from the Father, and that love between them which is the Holy Spirit—and the (if possible) even more staggering implications of the doctrine of the Incarnation—that at some precise historical moment the Word took flesh and dwelt among us. There are finally the immense implications of the idea of Revelation, that the eternal God chose to reveal something of Himself to us and that we therefore have knowledge of this transcendent, eternal realm in a way which infinitely surpasses all merely human glimpses of eternity.

There is an immense gamble here, as there is with regard

to the Church's stance of dogmatic certitude, because if this assertion concerning eternity is deemed incredible, then the Church's entire existence is rendered inauthentic. It cannot be rescued by appeals to its supposed practical or worldly utility.

But, on the other hand, if this teaching is true, then it is the most significant statement about our existence with which we will ever be confronted. One cannot be indifferent to the possibility of eternity, nor, having once accepted it truly, can its existence fail to continually cast beams of the brightest light into our darkness. Those who are disciples of the Incarnate Word and who believe in His promises necessarily must see all aspects of existence differently. Conversely, those who lack this faith must necessarily be seen as lacking essential understanding of the nature of human existence.

The question immediately arises: Are those who do not believe to be consigned to perdition? Are they debarred from leading good and meaningful human lives? The answer is of course no, and it has been a positive aspect of the development of modern Christianity that it has enabled us to see this fact. There is also an advantage in our being enabled to see that there is a distinction to be made (although not a separation) between religion and morality, heretical though that proposition may seem to some people. Put crudely, there is a great deal about religion which is not useful in any discernible or measurable sense.

Kierkegaard, a Protestant whose writings I found inspiring and very helpful at one point in my life, distinguished the category of faith from the category of the ethical and dared to suggest that God's demand that Abraham sacrifice his son Isaac was a manifestation of pure faith, of pure response to the greatness and authority of God transcending all ethical notions. Ultimately, although I find it tempting, I do not think this can be true, and it is certainly not a Catholic idea. But there is a kernel of truth in it.

What contemporary Christianity is most in danger of losing sight of is what might be called the esthetic dimension of religion—the fact that genuine religion ultimately means a

human response to what is recognized as great, holy, powerful, good, and beautiful. As with art, a much lesser instance
of the same kind of experience, this response is not primarily
useful. It is indeed useless, because it is primarily recognition,
response, acknowledgment. It tends to express itself in praise,
but often it is silent and even immobile before the thing perceived. In ultimate terms contemplation has primacy over action.

I do not think historical Catholicism can be fairly accused
of discouraging activity in the world, or of fostering the idea
that ethics and religion have nothing to do with one another.
In fact, some of the most powerful attacks against the
Church, especially at the time of the Reformation, were
directed against its alleged overemphasis on good works. Catholicism is in some ways a very pragmatic religion, always
tending to form organizations, to throw up structures, to provide work for people to do.

But its real greatness lies in its sustained ability, over many
centuries and in so many cultures and climates, to keep alive
in men's hearts the sense of eternity and the sense of the reality of the all-powerful and all-loving God. The "useless" response to the beauty and greatness of God is what we call
worship, and the Church has masterfully created conditions
in all times and places in which worship can occur.

The dissatisfaction with Catholic worship which has been
so marked a feature of postconciliar times has much to do
with the prevailing dissatisfaction with the idea of worship itself. Catholic ritual has been criticized not because it is not
an effective vehicle for worship but because it *is*—what certain
modern people object to is a ritual which is "for God" rather
than "for me."

Next to dogma, the word ritual is probably that aspect of
the Catholic phenomenon most guaranteed to provoke negative responses, and the term "meaningless ritual" is now itself
routinely employed as a meaningless ritual, as though all ritual were meaningless.

But it is again enlightening to recall how recently—as recently as fifteen years ago—traditional Catholic ritual was

deemed to be one of the Church's strongest points, the source of a great deal of its appeal among both simple and sophisticated people. In the practical order, it was ritual which perhaps better than anything else gave to many people, including some who came to it as unbelievers, a sense of the reality of eternity, of the beauty and majesty of God, and of the possibility of an appropriate human response to God.

Ritual becomes meaningless in one of two ways—by people ceasing to believe in those things which the ritual is meant to effect and symbolize, or by their expecting from the ritual the kind of pragmatic effects which it was never intended to bring about. The first danger is that of estheticism, a heresy which can be devastating in its consequences but fortunately tends to be confined to rather small elements of the population. The second, now at least, is much more widespread.

To me, authentic Catholic ritual reverberates with intimations of eternity, and it has had this aspect for me for as long as I can remember. As does dogma, ritual presents a world larger, deeper, and richer than that of our experience. It summons and focuses our attention, however briefly, on eternity. When either dogma or ritual is thought of as necessarily leading to certain practical results—a greater human sensitivity, for example, or a new dedication to helping others—it is misconceived. The connection is short-circuited. The rich stew is once again reduced to the soup of the day.

The sacramental religion which is Catholicism seems to me the only kind appropriate to the Incarnation, and as a consequence I have never been particularly attracted to the Protestant churches. But the sacraments have meaning only as vessels of eternal life, not as mere venerable and dramatic ceremonies or as expressions of present human needs and triumphs. If we represent them as anything other than what they are, we effectively cheat people.

In our time there are many people who accept the importance of ritual in the abstract but in effect ask why we need these particular rituals. They are offended by the seemingly arbitrary nature of a prescribed ritual, when it seems to them that there are many ways available to improve it, or even to make use of original liturgical compositions.

The "arbitrary" character of Catholicism, and indeed of all of Christianity, seems to me something very basic to it and something which must be accepted and recognized. It is a character imparted by Catholicism's being a historical religion. For if the objection were taken far enough, we would have to ask in effect why God chose to become man at the particular time and place He did. Most of us could probably conceive of other times and places, perhaps even other personages, which would seem to us more appropriate for the Incarnation and more conducive to its effects. The Church itself represents a similar "scandal of particularity," and throughout history it has been the repeated contention of the Church's critics and enemies that Christ could not have founded a Church like this one, by which they mean that He ought not to have.

Anything which is historical, and which is allowed to have its true historical character, developing organically through time, comes to have a circumscribed and particular identity which it cannot lose and is not free to surrender. The scandal of particularity which begins by questioning why the Church's rituals need to be observed in this particular arbitrary way, or why certain dogmas are expressed in this form rather than in some other, soon moves on to wondering why it is not possible to have a Church quite different from this one. The final point of such speculation, at which some have already arrived, is to question the once-and-for-all character of God's sending His Divine Son. Could there not be many such incarnations, in many different cultures? Given certain assumptions, it becomes virtually necessary to think so.

Paradoxically, it seems to me that the "arbitrary" character of Catholicism is precisely what saves it from being truly arbitrary. Of course the Son of God could have been incarnated under different conditions. Of course we might have a Church different from the one we have. Of course our rituals or our dogmas might have taken quite different form. But in the order of history they have not. God has somehow willed them to be what they are.

Romanticism has been defined as "split religion," and in the past few years there has been a "rediscovery" of religion by people who were previously indifferent or hostile to it. However, it is a discovery which is basically inimical to Christianity precisely because it has to do with religion in general, while Christianity, as an incarnational and historical faith, is very much religion in particular. A church which allows free expression to all manner of doctrinal, liturgical, and moral impulses is a church which soon falls victim to the spirit of the age. It becomes a vehicle for the expression of the favored "religious" impulses of a particular culture, but to that very extent it can no longer lay claim to being the proper expression of divine revelation. It ceases to be a revealed religion. It becomes a primarily worldly entity, echoing and re-echoing the world's voices.

Thus far I have said little very specifically about tradition, but I think its presence is detectable in everything I have said. There is a specific danger in intertwining the arguments for the importance of tradition and the truth of Christianity, just as there is a specific danger in emphasizing the esthetic character of religion. Paralleling the heresy of estheticism is the heresy of traditionalism, in which whatever is old is deemed good and in which the preservation of historic Christianity is necessary because Christianity is one of the foundation stones on which civilization is built. For a Catholic, the assertion of truth is something to which we must return again and again.

However, it also seems to me that the traditionalism of the Catholic Church is no accident, and for several reasons. First, to be a historical religion means not only that the Catholic faith develops through time but also that it looks back, unabashedly, for its validation and its source somewhere in the past, embarrassing though this notion may be to some people. If we take the Incarnation seriously, then we must accept the fact that the high point of human history is a specific event which can be dated and located with a fair degree of precision. Our "story," such as we have, is essentially the fleshing out of that story. We look forward to Christ's coming again, but equally we look backward to His having already come. We are barred from being the "now generation."

There is a cheap kind of traditionalism in which outdated language and dress, musty old buildings, and old-fashioned ideas conjure up a sense of permanence and stability. This is not the kind of traditionalism which Catholicism can countenance, although from time to time attempts are made to co-opt it for that purpose. However, it is also appropriate that the Church should seem, from the world's viewpoint, an unnaturally stable and even outdated institution. For the Church, if it truly speaks from the perspective of eternity, must always manage to distance itself from the prevailing spirit of each particular age, must always speak in ways which will strike the world as strange. And in the process of its long historical development, it is also inevitable that the Church will discover certain forms of expression—verbal, symbolical, or institutional—which it will recognize as having enduring and permanent validity and which it will continue from age to age. (Put another way, not every age is equally penetrating in its religious understanding or creative in its expressions of that understanding. My feeling is that our own age is particularly impoverished, especially in its sense of liturgical and symbolic expression.)

But what then are we to make of hierarchy? It can be defended in terms of tradition, but I think it is necessary to give it a more solid gounding than that. I am not among those who regard religion as a quasi-aristocratic phenomenon which ordinary people cannot be trusted to understand and which must be upheld by the "leaders" of society in the same way that, for example, the value of high art is so upheld. In fact I think the history of Catholicism shows a religion which penetrated very deeply into the life of the common people, a situation which endured until after the Second Vatican Council. That there has occurred an estrangement of elite from masses in the postconciliar Church, I think has been due largely to the determination of some of the elite to move farther and faster than most ordinary believers were willing to do.

However, since the Church speaks from the perspective of eternity, it is true that democracy, like all other political systems, is essentially irrelevant to its life. It is free to incorporate elements of the democratic system into its structure, as it has generally incorporated elements of whatever political system has prevailed at any particular time, but it is not obligated to do so. Hence the continued existence of a hierarchical system is no embarrassment to the Church and can even be taken as a laudable sign of its independence from prevailing customs.

Hierarchy as it functions in the Church can be conceived in at least two ways. One is hierarchy as principality and privilege, the system whereby bishops and other prelates live in luxury and require that a kind of servile deference be paid to them. Clearly this is the remnant of the cultural mores of certain past ages and has no relevance to our own time.

However, it is also true that the problem of hierarchical authority cannot be solved by an easy appeal to the "authority of service" or other concepts devised to help avoid the hard questions. The bishop remains, in the root meaning of his title, an overseer. He is not merely a presiding officer or chairman, still less a kindly grandfather who always praises and never scolds. If the Church claims to teach truth, it cannot avoid the question of where the authentic power to articulate that truth lies. Catholic doctrine and tradition concede the key role in the process to the bishops, individually and collectively, and classical theories of popular consensus, as developed by Cardinal Newman, for example, necessarily limit the role of that consensus. Any bishop who truly seeks to do his duty in times as disturbed and confused as our own will find ample occasions to warn, correct, and teach with authority. For some, this necessary exercise of office will inevitably seem tyrannical and oppressive.

So far I have talked of "Catholicism" in terms general enough to apply to Eastern Orthodoxy and to Anglo-Catholicism as well as to the Church of Rome. In fact I have a good deal of sympathy for the view of Catholicism which defines it widely enough to encompass these other churches and which speaks of Catholic Christianity in terms of the identity which emerged during the first four or five centuries of the Church's history.

But the papacy still looms very large and, contrary to what many people feel, for me it looms even larger in our own day. If we accept historical development in the Church, then we must accept the fact that with every development certain doors are shut for the future, even as other doors may be opened. The papal office is one such door. The full maturation of the papal office has shut many doors even as it has opened others. Following the First Vatican Council, and following what the Second Vatican Council said about papal authority, it is not possible to pretend that the papal primacy is not integral to Catholicism or that its development is reversible.

A decade ago I was inclined to minimize the importance of that office, since I believed that whatever was essential to Catholicism was found in conciliar decrees as well as in the general traditions of the Church. In the meantime, however, I have come to a deepened appreciation of the importance of the papacy, and in fact I regard it as indispensable to the future of Christianity.

Eastern Orthodoxy and the worldwide Anglican communion are the essential test cases for the viability of a Catholicism which rests on the consensus of the whole Church, expressed primarily through the collective body of the episcopacy. Orthodoxy seems to preserve this Catholicity very well. However, it is so closely tied to ethnic identities that it is difficult to judge how well it would survive independent of those identities. Unlike Roman Catholicism, it has not attempted to penetrate to all corners of the world or to bring into its fold all those, of whatever diverse nations, races, cultures, who will listen to its teachings. Anglicanism, meanwhile, seems increasingly vulnerable to modernism in all its forms, a fact which is especially notable in its moral teachings. Despite staunch pockets of orthodoxy within its ample

folds, Anglicanism seems vulnerable to modernistic on-
slaughts at its highest levels of leadership, including many of
its bishops.

I agree with those commentators who identify *Humanae
Vitae*, the 1968 encyclical on contraception and related matters issued by Pope Paul VI, as an important watershed in
the history of attitudes towards the papacy. However, unlike
most of those who make this point in order to argue that the
encyclical was a disaster from the point of view of papal credibility, I think that in the long run the prestige of the papal
office will be immensely enhanced by it.

Having said that, I must confess to having been among
those who were made unhappy by its original issuance and
who hoped that somehow a "compromise" settlement could
have been worked out. But much has happened in ten years'
time, and it is becoming more and more clear (and frighten-
ingly so) what the full implications are of an attitude which
deliberately divorces human sexual activity from the purposes
of procreation.

Looking merely at the history of the papacy in the twentieth century, I find it highly impressive that, although the wisdom or advisability of this or that practical papal policy
might be questioned, on matters of formal teaching ranging
from sex to social justice, as well as more general doctrinal
questions, the popes have been unerring in their understanding of the real issues at stake and their courageous willingness to speak even when their speaking has predictably
provoked a storm of abusive protest. While "the institutional
Church" is often dismissed as stodgy, cautious, and mired in
routine, I find on the contrary that the popes have been and
continue to be truly prophetic. Where the Roman Catholic
Church would be without the strong, balanced Catholic
sense of Pope Paul VI, I find impossible to imagine.

The mention of *Humanae Vitae* leads immediately to that
remaining characteristic of historic Catholicism which I
identified earlier as essential to it—namely, its clear and well-
defined moral teaching; and it is precisely because of those
teachings, especially those having to do with sexual behavior,

that the Church is now under such severe attack from so many quarters and is in fact actively hated.

It is often said that the preconciliar Church overemphasized sexual morality, and that may well have been true on the practical level, although attention to the papal encyclicals of the past century would suggest that this imbalance did not affect the highest levels of Church leadership. In the abstract it is easy to say that sexual sins are less serious than matters of social injustice, yet sex has a way of continually intruding itself into public consciousness. It is a subject that will not go away, mainly because our sexual identity and the behavior which flows from it is so basic to all our personalities and all of us feel that sexual rights and wrongs have a lot to do with who we are and who we ought to be.

It is not possible to discuss the complexities of the sexual revolution in this short space. However, I think that what goes by that name is based on a whole series of false assumptions about human nature and the nature of morality, assumptions which cannot help but result in disasters for those who make them, and ultimately for the whole society within which they are made. It seems to me that authentic Catholic teaching about sex in our times reveals a wisdom, a sanity, and a balance which "the world" sadly lacks and many other religious bodies seem eager to throw away as quickly as possible. (Absent a hierarchy, and especially a papacy, the Church of Rome might be easily stampeded in the same direction.)

Preconciliar Catholics are also often accused of having been overly sin-conscious, our religion too negative and built upon notions of guilt. Again, in the practical order this may well have been true for some people, although I am convinced that it is a reality which has been greatly exaggerated for sensationalistic purposes. There are several dimensions of the question which are commonly ignored, however. One is the fact that, however much the Church may be accused of having exaggerated the element of moral guilt, this very exaggeration was a compliment to human nature, by its attributing of moral responsibility to man. Free will was taken seriously, which meant that both sanctity and damnation were regarded as real possibilities, within reach of all. Human actions and human decisions had real moral weight. The new spirit of "liberation," while it talks a great deal about maturity and adulthood, often ends by casting people in the role of permanent adolescents, who are never fully responsible for what they do but are constantly excused and indulged.

Traditional Catholic moral theology, including the often excoriated casuistry, seems to me to have been based on an acute realism about human nature and a nicely wrought balance between a clear-eyed awareness of what people are prone to do on the one hand and what they are capable of on the other. The moral law as explicated by the Catholic Church was always a nice balance between justice and mercy. For many generations of people it made the reality of moral choice, and the drama of that choice, immediate and real, just as it made the prospect of eternity, and of an incarnate Second Person of the Trinity, immediate and real.

In the postconciliar Church much energy has gone into the task of refashioning Catholicism in such a way that no one can be harmed by it, that none of the distortions and deformations which are alleged to have been so common a feature of the preconciliar Church can ever recur. Such an enterprise, while the motives behind it are understandable, seems to me profoundly misconceived. For a religion which contains within it no possible sources of deformation, which does not harbor elements which can be misused for destruction, is also a religion incapable of any very profound good. It is a religion which is simply weak and impotent.

Historically the Church has always been aware of the possibility of such deformations, of scrupulosity, for example. But it has, in its divine origins and its sense of historic mission, chosen to hazard this possibility. Without the possibility of hate, there is no love. Without the danger of despair there can be no hope. Without sin there is no redemption. The Church which seeks to uncover in people the image and likeness of their Creator, to point out to them the path of imitation of their Savior, must demand a great deal and, like a great surgeon, always confront the possibility that the operation will fail, that the patient will emerge worse for the experience.

In summary, Catholicism seems to me unique in the world today in the consistency with which it has made vivid and accessible the prospect of eternal life and of life in the world lived in the light of eternity. Its worldly achievements, including its actions on behalf of social justice, are not inconsiderable. But it is not for this primarily that it lays claim to distinction. Religion in its root meaning is a binding, a process by which individuals surrender themselves to something greater than themselves, something worthy of their surrender. It is an all-or-nothing proposition in which salvation is at stake. For nearly two millennia the Roman Catholic Church has mediated this awareness to the world, in innumerable and varied ways. The crisis through which it is now passing is one of the three greatest in its history, along with the Arian crisis of the fourth century and the Reformation of the sixteenth. It is part of an authentic Catholic faith to be confident that, however much it may be buffeted in this crisis, however deeply wounded, it will not only survive but emerge stronger. For if God's ways are not our ways, then His ways for His Church are likewise not ours, and its future is already determined, not by what we do to this Church, or fail to do for it, but by His own plan for it and the destiny with which He endowed it from its very foundation.

AT HOME IN THE CHURCH

CANDIDA LUND

A Dominican nun, Sister Candida is a native Chicagoan and received her B.A. from Rosary College there and her Ph.D. in political science from the University of Chicago. She served for a time on the research staff of Secretary of the Treasury Henry Morgenthau and then turned to teaching. She became chairman of the Department of Political Science at Rosary in 1961 and has been president of the college since 1964. She has written magazine articles, contributed an article on Saint Joan to *Saints for All Seasons*, and edited a collection of prayers for today's women, *The Days and the Nights*. She has received numerous academic awards, including a Doctor of Letters *honoris causa* from Lincoln College. She serves on the board of directors of the Thomas More Association, the American Council on Education, and the Carnegie Foundation.

Why am I still a Catholic? It is the adverb that intrigues me
when the question is posed in this fashion. It is the adverb
that for me provides the challenge. The Age of Aquarius is
over, and we are living in the Age of the Adverb—the story of
our times can be told in adverbs that mirror flux. Let me give
examples. X *currently* is married to Y. Has he left the priesthood *yet?* My children don't go to church *any more. For-
merly* she was a nun. They're not married, *merely* living together. *Now,* anything goes. The more things appear to
change, the more they do change, the French to the contrary.

In the latter part of 1977 a comedy by Mary O'Malley,
Once a Catholic (again the adverb), was presented by the
Royal Court Theatre in London. Perhaps a collection of writings with the theme "Why Catholic" might also be looked
upon as comedy if one were willing to use the conception of
comedy developed from Roman comedy by postclassical critics. This conception regarded comedy as a form capable of
inspiring morality as well as mirth. Its function was to teach
and delight by exhibiting a picture of ordinary, unheroic persons and events in a suitably low style of writing.

Twenty-five years ago the question "Why are you still a
Catholic?" would not have been raised. Convert autobi-
ographies were alive and well in the first half of the twentieth
century, as evidenced by Karl Stern's *Pillar of Fire,* Dorothy
Day's *From Union Square to Rome,* and Thomas Merton's
Seven Storey Mountain, but these works, typical of the genre,
explained why people "entered the Church," not why they
remained.

Had I been asked thirty-five years ago to answer why I was a Catholic, my approach would have been different. I would have approached the task like a Brunhilde or Boadicea, the warrior-woman proudly a part of the Church Militant. In some measure, this was due to my education.

During my senior year in high school I was introduced to apologetics and loved it. In part, I think it was the ring of the word, a word I had never heard before. It spoke to me of something lofty and intellectual—and I thought it fitted me for battle. Later, in a college logic class, I experienced a similar excitement when I learned of St. Thomas Aquinas' Five Proofs for the existence of God. (I always thought of them in upper case, not lower.) That not all great minds had succumbed to these trenchant proofs raised no problem. With them, I was girded—and goaded—further. I welcomed the opportunity to talk about my faith. How could anyone resist crystal-clear proofs and remain outside The Fold?

Undoubtedly I experienced my greatest surge of this kind of feeling in college. Not for me was the Kantian notion that religion is a private affair and that all attempts to influence the opinion of others in such matters could be regarded as impertinent and overbearing.

It was during the summers following my sophomore and junior years that, spurred by a modicum of proper zeal and, less loftily, by a secret yen to play the part of Major Barbara in Catholic guise, I did Catholic Evidence work (translate: street preaching) in Oklahoma. One might say that it had all begun with Frank Sheed and the indomitable Maisie in Hyde Park the decade before. London's Hyde Park, however, was a far cry from the small, dusty, sun-scorched Oklahoma towns in the forties where, if the residents had ever seen a mad dog, certainly they had never seen an Englishman. The British listeners that clustered around the Sheeds were not prototypes of the "Okies" who encircled the five students from Rosary College. Audiences in both locations, on the other hand, had a common mark: They were lightly peppered with hecklers, and it is these who give flavor, generally, to an outdoor performance.

We were there to bring to people in the streets some facts about the Catholic Church. We also hoped to eradicate some prejudices.

Our schedule called for two- to four-night stands in rural towns. We announced ourselves the day before by nailing up homemade posters—"all you want to know about the Catholic Church." On the appointed nights we drew our crowds by playing records of a deceptively rollicking nature over our public-address system. "The Beer Barrel Polka" and "Take Me Out to the Ball Game" hardly gave indication of what was to follow. Attracting a crowd was not difficult. The people welcomed a break in their usual monotonous pattern, and they were curious about us as well as about the Catholic Church. We were not competing with television or air conditioning.

In each town, we followed the same format. First, ten minutes of popular music, then we "preachers" gathered around our miniature portable organ and wavered through "Come Holy Ghost," a ghastly, not ghostly, experience for one, like me, unable to sing. The "Our Father" followed and the salute to the flag. One of us greeted the crowd and explained that we had come from suburban Chicago because we had heard that Oklahomans were among the most religious in the United States, and we wished to tell them about our religion. Two talks were given—a forty-minute one and a twenty-minute one. (Attention spans were longer in the forties.) Our platform was the back of a pickup truck. Among our subjects were the life of Christ, the Blessed Mother, the Church, confession, prayer, and purgatory.

After the talks we answered questions. Because some of our listeners had been weaned on lurid tales of the Maria Monk ilk, it was not surprising that their queries reflected this. Furthermore, sex seems to be more interesting to most people than theology. There were generally some raunchy questions on human sexuality—centering often on priests and sisters—understandably not considered four decades later by the Catholic Theological Society. We, of course, handled such questions in proper Victorian fashion.

In closing, to show our patriotism, sometimes doubted, we played "God Bless America" and "The Star-Spangled Banner." Through it all, the refrain that kept resounding within me was the old Catholic Action song written by Father Lord, "An Army of Youth flying the standard of truth. Catholic Action our only cry." Pacific militancy could not fail to triumph!

Now, however, in explaining why I am still a Catholic, I feel no need of a triumphal approach. I feel no truculence. I feel no urgency for a so-called reasoned position, although I like to think that I am not totally dependent upon Pascal's heart which has reasons that the mind knows naught of.

My reasons, reasonably or not, work for me. They reflect my training as a political scientist as much as my early upbringing—perhaps even more. My reasons for still being a Catholic are: (1) I treasure my Catholic heritage. (2) I like the company I keep. (3) I believe in institutions. (4) I am helped by the Church's moral code. (5) I am provided with a perspective. (6) For me, Christ is central. I do not say that my reasons would necessarily prove persuasive to others. Nor do I deny that it would be possible to adjust some of them to buttress the position of one of a different persuasion. I also recognize that to an extent my reasons are interwoven. I do not see how they could be otherwise.

1. I Treasure My Catholic Heritage

When I visited Greece several years ago, I was struck by the curiously hallowed atmosphere that still envelopes Delphi. In the old city of Jerusalem I was deeply moved standing before the Western Wall less than three weeks after the Six Day War had again opened it to Jews after nineteen years. I watched Jews from many countries stream in and insert into the cracks of this symbolic wall (the last remnant of the compound of Solomon's Temple) kvittels, prayers of petition written in a cramped hand upon tightly rolled, minuscule pieces of paper. In both places, no matter how sympathetic I felt, however, I was a spectator—indeed, almost a stranger.

But Chartres is mine, as is Le Corbusier's Ronchamp chapel and Matisse's glorious chapel of Notre Dame du Rosaire at Vence. It makes no difference that more than seven hundred years separate the first from the latter two. In all three I am equally at home, for they belong to me. They are a part of my inheritance.

The scope of my Catholic heritage goes beyond churches. It includes music, prayer, art, literature—all that is creative. Nor is my heritage limited to the grand scale. There is for me a more personal heritage, perhaps less now a part of my life, but still with me. It was built upon such things as my mother's splashing us with holy water on a stormy night, or tucking under my pillow a piece of palm saved from the last Palm Sunday, or saying, "offer it up for the Poor Souls," whether "it" was a skinned knee or a disappointment, major in the life of a small child. Different Catholic families have different ways, but these ways help to constitute a heritage.

Heritage provides badly needed continuity, and continuity nurtures roots. Even before Alex Haley flashed upon the scene, the young—both black and white—were searching consciously and unconsciously for roots or, to put it another way, an identification with the past. Such an identification helps young people answer the critical question, "Who am I?" Joan Baez sang, "I gotta be me." Fine, as long as you know who me is.

To let such a heritage be dissipated is a mistake. At the same time, one does not want one's faith encrusted with anachronisms. I do not want the Church to be a museum piece. Yet a kindly rationale for the nibbling away at certain traditions can prove helpful. Each one who has been "brought up Catholic" probably mourns the official discard of some practice. I shall always be piqued at the unnecessarily harsh way the Church scrapped St. Christopher. Little difference that he never existed. He did not need to. It was the legend of Christopher that was important. It was what he symbolized that was inspirational. No wonder Anne Morrow Lindbergh wrote of him:

Christopher, come back to earth again.
There is no age in history when men
So cried for you, Saint of a midnight wild. . . .

Another irritation has been the shifting of the feast of the Epiphany from January 6 to a floating date. Did those who wantonly destroyed Twelfth Night realize what they had done to a whole body of literature, to say nothing of the Partridge in the Pear Tree?

It is well to stress that proper appreciation of one's heritage does not result in divisiveness, bigots to the contrary. In the first place, the kind of heritage of which I am writing is not exclusive domain. Fortunately! It is ironic that Gregorian chant is a part of the required course of study at St. John's College (not church-related) in Annapolis, whereas on Catholic campuses one could search vainly for a student who could tell the difference between a punctum and a torculus.

It is through cherishing my own heritage that I have been helped to regard with appreciation the heritages of others. I once heard Gregory Baum say that it is in our particularity that we find our universality. From experience I find this so.

2. I Like the Company I Keep

In recent decades from time to time certain well-known people, to show disapproval, have resigned from clubs whose bylaws or charters discriminated against particular minorities. There is a reverse situation: the willingness, or longing, to be identified with an institution whose members are admired. Obviously, this could not mean all members. Such could only be in Voltaire's Dr. Pangloss's best of all possible worlds.

In the Catholic Church I can easily find a number of people in heaven and on earth who leave me jubilant that, with them, I am still a Catholic. I have always liked Woodrow Wilson's response to the gentleman who congratulated him upon appointing Justice Brandeis to the Supreme Court but added, "It's too bad Mr. Brandeis is a Jew." The President's reply was classic—and deservedly withering. He said, "Mr. Brandeis would not be Mr. Brandeis if he were not a Jew."

I have a small but select circle of heavenly friends whose Catholicism helped make them what they are (small because in picking my heavenly friends I look for compatibility). Here I shall write particularly about two: St. Joan of Arc and St. Thomas More. In my opinion, Joan of Arc would not be Joan of Arc had she not been a Catholic. Thomas More would not have been Thomas More had he not been a Catholic.

I was in my early teens when I first claimed them as friends. I was proud that we were part of the same Church. It gratifies me that both Joan of Arc and Thomas More have a freshness and force today. Biographies and plays about St. Joan continue to pour forth five centuries after her death. Richard Bolt with his drama and film *A Man for All Seasons* assured More's introduction to countless people to whom he had been unknown or little known.

St. Joan was, as I have written elsewhere, an earthy visionary, not a usual combination. She was fortunately more woman than lady, and that pleases me. I have always preferred my saints to be women and my sinners to be ladies. This is a bit akin to Shaw's manner of making his rogues heroic and Brecht's his examplars rogues. Joan's virtues were warm, human virtues writ large. She possessed purposefulness, piety, salty wit, naturalness, shrewdness, courage, clear thinking, confidence in God, leadership, strong-mindedness, a high sense of duty, and a love of freedom. She was able to put in tandem God and practical affairs, whether political or military.

The transcript of her trial carries her explanation to the judges of why she knew how to act before the king. She was told, she said, by her voices, "Go boldly: When thou art before the king he shall have a good sign to receive and believe in thee." Go boldly she did, and provided for all time a motto of courage for women to adopt.

Joan of Arc and Thomas More in many ways were much alike in spite of pronounced differences. Many of Joan's virtues were also More's. Both were the good servants of their kings, yet both had to tussle with this role. On the other hand, their upbringings were vastly different; hers, simple and rustic; his, sophisticated and urban. She had no desire to marry, indeed even took to court a suitor who claimed she had breached a contract to marry him, and won her case. More married twice. Joan could not write her name. More gave us some of the most important writing in the sixteenth century, and saw that his daughter Meg was well instructed in Greek and Latin. Joan could not bear the loss of her freedom—not to be able to roam the countryside—and preferred death to imprisonment. More valued his imprisonment in the Tower of London. From it he wrote Meg, "Our Lord be thanked, I am in good health of body and in good quiet of mind; and of worldly things I no more desire than I have." The fact that Joan was only eighteen when she was first put in prison and More was in his mid-fifties might account in part for their contrasting attitudes.

Both had penetrating wits, hers down-to-earth, his urbane. At her trial, Joan was asked whether the voice of St. Margaret spoke to her in English. "Why should she speak English? She is not on the English side," was her answer. To the question whether St. Michael was naked when he appeared to her, she replied, "Do you think God has not wherewithal to clothe him?"

St. Thomas More, as befits a man always merry and loving with his family and friends, jested with his executioner. Because of physical weakness caused by his long imprisonment he sought aid as he ascended the scaffold steps, asking, "I pray you see me safely up. As for my coming down, I shall shift for myself." He delayed the execution to arrange his beard so that it would not be cut with his head since it had committed no treason.

The company I like is not confined to those like Joan and Thomas More who are a part of the Communion of Saints. There are living people who make me proud that "we go to the same Church": Mother Teresa of India, Dorothy Day, Cesar Chavez, Senator Mansfield, Father Dominique Pire. But these are the recognized. There are also the unsung who leave me glad we share the Church. Some of them I see when I go to Mass at St. Patrick's Cathedral in New York or Chicago's Holy Name or, indeed, Mass anywhere. They are the boozy old tramps asleep in the pews, the "bag ladies" who are there getting warm, the young mothers sometimes big with child, the husbands worrying about their families, the concerned worrying about the world. In short, the common woman and the common man as well as the not-so-common woman and the not-so-common man.

This is the company I like to keep and that helps me to feel at home in the Church. The old Baltimore Catechism would put it a shorter way: It would say this is the Church holy and the Church universal.

3. I Believe in Institutions

I believe in institutions because, properly structured and regulated, they help to provide order and growth where otherwise there would be chaos. This is no longer as widely recognized as it once was and as it should be. Unfortunately, in the last decade or so institutions have had a bad press; no institution more than the Catholic Church. It seems to me that this stems, in large measure, from obfuscation of language. Institutions are too often condemned by those unaware of what institutions really are. For instance, some people say that they are disenchanted with the institutional church. The statement is tautological since there is no noninstitutional church. The Dutch Catechism cannot produce such a church. No one can. George Fox, the founder of the Quakers, did not believe in institutional religion, but would anyone today deny that Quakerism is an institution? In order to discuss institutions properly, a realization of what is meant by institutions is needed. (And this in turn might help to pinpoint the disenchantment.)

The Encyclopedia of Social Sciences, a bible of the social scientists, sheds some light on institutions, although the non-social scientist may regard the light as no more than fifteen watts. The encyclopedia declares that "our culture is a synthesis—or at least an aggregation—of institutions, each of which has its own domain and its distinctive office. The function of each is to set a pattern of behavior and to fix a zone of tolerance for an activity or a complement of activities."

In an attempt to get closer to a definition, it also suggests that "it [institution] connotes a way of thought or action of some prevalence and permanence, which is embedded in the habits of a group or the customs of a people."

In this light one can raise the question whether it would be possible to live without institutions. Aristotle had a word to say on the matter with regard to a primary institution. He wrote that the man who could live without a state must be either a god or a beast. Even Paul Goodman in *Growing Up Absurd* recognizes that children growing up must have institutions of work, play, citizenship, and family, for it is these that will give scope to their native gifts.

The term institution, regrettably, sets up a scapegoat. When I disapprove of something, I can smear it by saying that it is "institutional." Woodrow Wilson pierced this subterfuge when he inscribed a copy of his book *The State* for a friend. On the flyleaf he wrote, "A book of bones and anatomy. The real life of institutions is in men and measures." Expressions used to describe particular institutions point up such an assertion: Holy Mother Church, Alma Mater, Mother Russia, John Bull, Uncle Sam.

The Catholic Church is one of the oldest, largest, and most significant worldwide institutions. In its twenty centuries of existence it has been reverenced and reviled, lauded and loathed. It has possibly been shaken but certainly never shattered.

As a Catholic I am pleased at the good the Catholic Church has accomplished. It has done this not only supernaturally through God's grace, but naturally because it is an institution. It has many ministries. It cares for the sick and the aged. In 1977 there were, in the United States, 730 general and special hospitals with 170,145 beds. In 461 homes for the aged, 52,230 persons were receiving care. Two hundred and nineteen orphanages and havens were housing 15,974 children. The number of students under Catholic instructions was 8,751,901. It is recognized that the Catholic school system cares for a disproportionately high number of the urban poor, a number large enough to cause reconsideration of denied government aid. There were 432,597 students in 245 Catholic colleges and universities. Statistics have little warmth, but they reveal a story, understated rather than exaggerated.

Less possible to pinpoint statistically is the Church's service to the poor—not enough but still in considerable measure. Its influence, too, upon the family has been important. In each of these areas its accomplishments have touched the lives of those who are not Catholic in addition to those who are. Because there remains much to do is no reason for failing to recognize what has been done.

Since the death of Pope John we have seen no great encyclicals, but I cannot forget as a college student in the forties how I was still being stirred by the fearless social encyclicals that had begun with Leo XIII's *Condition of Labor*. He had beaten the American Congress by several decades in his advocacy of social reform for the workers. In 1891 he wrote, "To sum up, then, We may lay it down as a general and lasting law that workingmen's associations should be so organized and governed as to furnish the best and most suitable means for attaining what is aimed at; that is to say, for helping each individual member to better his condition to the utmost in body, mind, and property."

In short, I regard the Catholic Church as a great civilizing force helping to provide growth and order. It is an institution worthy of respect and regard—and of my allegiance. But as I write this I do not wish to appear uncritical. There are practices which I decry—not many, but some regrettable, perhaps even deplorable. Ronald Knox could not have been only jesting when he said that if one is going to travel on the barque of Peter, he had better not look too closely into the engine room. Machiavellian politics have never been confined to the secular state, nor to Machiavelli's own century. From time to time, one finds in the Church sins of omission as well as commission, unnatural narrowness, and missed opportunities.

The Church's Janus-like approach troubles those who are

not Catholics as well as some who are. As one who is not a Catholic, George Anastaplo wrote in his book *Human Being and Citizen*:

> Another instance that disturbs many good men today is the teaching of the Roman Catholic Church with respect to birth control. If its prohibition of certain means of birth control were regarded by the Church as is, say, a requirement that meat not be eaten on Friday that would be one thing—and, indeed, some restraints could even be salutary in some places, or at some times, if only to induce human beings to reflect upon the natural order of things and the role of sexual activity in it. But when the teaching is insisted upon (with an effect on public policy) as a universal and unalterable dictate of natural law—which would be binding on all right-thinking men and women, not Roman Catholics alone— serious problems arise. . . .

> Thus the Roman Catholic teachers who have done so much to keep alive the natural law tradition among us may, by their evident disregard of considerations of prudence, be inhibiting others, in a world beset by unprecedented population growth, from taking that tradition seriously.

On the other hand, Professor Anastaplo credits the Church with important thinking on the morality of war. He writes, "But in another realm which has to do with deliberations about the prospects and conduct of another world war, Roman Catholic thinkers seem to be among the leaders bringing to bear on a new problem some old teachings. Even notorious Marxists have praised papal statements on this subject."

Professor Anastaplo's remarks carry a perverse compliment. They would not be made about an institution that lacked standing. (Such a statement may sound a little like an author saying that he would rather have a bad review in the New York *Times* than no review at all.) Because the Catholic Church is an institution capable of monumental impact for good, decent men and women watch it with interest and concern. They look to it for standards. They do not wish to see it falter or fail to achieve the good possible.

4. I Am Helped by the Church's Moral Code

When I say that one of the reasons I am still a Catholic is because I am helped by the Church's enunciation of its moral code, I am not implying that outside of the Catholic Church I would not be able to build a moral position. To hold this would be ludicrous.

Unquestionably, however, there would be for me greater obstacles if I tried alone to search for a moral code. The greatest difficulty in the search today results from the disrepute into which natural right has fallen. I doubt that most Catholics are aware of the battering natural right (or, to use its more Catholic term, natural law) has suffered. Now natural right and natural law seem to be used interchangeably, although the latter has theological underpinnings which the former has not. The leading twentieth-century student of the subject, Leo Strauss, wrote that by natural law "is meant a law that determines what is right and wrong and that has power or is valid by nature, inherently, hence everywhere and always."

Natural right's fall from grace took place earlier in German thought than in that of the rest of Western Europe and America. Nevertheless, unqualified relativism is now a part of Western thought in general if one excepts much of Catholic thought. The late Professor Strauss, Robert Maynard Hutchins Distinguished Service Professor of Political Science at the University of Chicago, wrote in *Natural Right and History*:

Present-day American social science, as far as it is not Roman Catholic social science, is dedicated to the proposition that all men are endowed by the evolutionary process or by a mysterious fate with many kinds of urges and aspirations, but certainly with no natural right.

Nevertheless, the need for natural right is as evident today as it has been for centuries and even millennia. To reject natural right is tantamount to saying that all right is positive right, and this means that what is right is determined exclusively by the legislators and the courts of the various countries.

This is not Olympian pondering of a remote academician. It is an expression of the deep concern of a thoughtful, but hardheaded, scholar, world-known, who recognized in the problem of natural right one of the most controversial and significant issues in contemporary political and social philosophy. Professor Strauss chose to teach in political-science departments rather than philosophy departments because he felt the action was in the former.

Natural Right and History was published in 1953. Other than realignments, twenty-five years later there is no pronounced change in American social science, nor is there a greater recognition of the need for natural right. Within political-science circles the efforts of Leo Strauss and others have brought some results. Papers on political philosophy are again being given at meetings of the American Political Science Association, and there are positions for professors of political philosophy on the faculties of colleges and universities. These developments show an unwillingness to accept the just as simply the legal.

Another realignment involves the numbers of Catholics who now reject a natural-law position and instead adopt doctrines of positivism and equate the just with the legal. On the other hand, it is the concern, conscious or unconscious, about positivism and relativism that has caused some young parents I know to abandon their positions as "cultural Catholics." Instead, they have become more closely identified with the Catholic Church so that their children will have the help of its ethical guidance. They do not wish their children to grow up thinking everything is relative. They want them to be introduced to some "absolutes." I also know former students who have again become more closely identified with things Catholic through their children, rather than because of them. In these instances the children have been the ones who have asked their parents to go to Mass with them, and who have clamored (with success) to go to Catholic schools.

Many parents I know are deeply disturbed by the environment in which their children are growing up. The response of a worried Chicago doctor who uprooted his large family and moved to Ireland is not a solution open to all. Probably it is not even a solution—the problem cannot be escaped. An increasing number of people do not even have familiarity with the rudimentary premise, avoid evil, do good.

"Avoid evil, do good" is disarmingly simple, but where does one go from there? Natural right is not easily discernible, and even with guidelines the search for virtue can be perplexing. One needs also to remember that guidelines are meant to help form consciences, not to supplant them nor to strait-jacket them.

I have ordinarily found the Church to have a healthy respect for the individual conscience, although it must be admitted that there have been times in history when churchmen trampled on the rights and consciences of Catholics. Recently at a friend's in Boston I came across a set of religion texts that I too had used in high school. The teaching on conscience was remarkably sound: "We are always bound to follow a certain conscience, even if false or erroneous. . . . Therefore, if we disobey a certain conscience we make ourselves responsible. . . . No authority, ecclesiastical or civil, can make it lawful for us to do what our conscience condemns as certainly wretched." Strong words! And not without their problems. The textbook was entitled *A Course in Religion for Catholic High Schools and Academies, Part III, Christian Morals.* It was written by Father John Laux more than forty years ago.

I am glad that the Church and its teachings have helped shape my conscience at the same time that it has not tried to destroy my reasoning. I need all the help I can get!

5. *I Am Provided with a Perspective*

A perspective makes a difference. The late Adlai Stevenson recognized this when he wrote poetically:

. . . here on the prairies of Illinois and the Middle
West, we can see a long way in all directions. We look
to east, to west, to north and south. . . . our ideas
come and go in all directions. Here there are no barriers,
no defenses, to ideas and inspirations. We want none;
we want no shackles of the mind or the spirit, no rigid
patterns of thought, no iron conformity.

To some, such a quotation may seem to have little application to a Church that burned Savonarola and Joan of Arc,
hounded Galileo, and as recently as my lifetime made life
difficult for Father John Courtney Murray and very difficult
for Teilhard de Chardin. Yet I find it applicable.

For one thing, the Church sees a long way. It is more concerned with Eternity than with the Now. Rightly understood,
it encourages looking in all directions. And although freedoms
are not absolutes, one should always realize within the
Church that the mind need not be shackled.

From the perspective with which my faith provides me,
several qualities flow, often in ways difficult to pinpoint except by reference to Now-cum-Eternity. One quality is
confidence. It has always seemed to me that encouraging
someone's confidence is one of the finest gifts to give.
Confidence wards off despair, and is an important evidence of
maturity. I can remember the spot where I was walking—the
midway of the University of Chicago—when I accepted without dismay that a lifetime would not be long enough to learn
all I wished to learn, but that I could still live happily.
Confidence makes such acceptance possible and even fruitful.

Confidence has a balance to keep it from becoming over-
confidence: moderation. This quality is for me best expressed
by negation in a little piece of doggerel that I remember from
my childhood:

Farewell, the hailstone cried, downward pelted,
How will the earth abide without me when I'm melted?

Perspective would have helped the hailstone.

A perspective is liberating. The unimportant things are

more likely to be recognized for what they are, and the important things come into their own. And as I see a long way in all directions, I think of one of the favorite themes of Baron von Hügel: the presence of truth in other religions. That good and reverent man wrote, "God has never left the world in complete and groping darkness; all religions contain some light from God."

While I was writing this chapter, a dear friend died as a result of an auto accident. A Dominican sister, she had been one of my professors when I was an undergraduate, and for more than twenty years we had been colleagues; but above all we were friends. Losing her made me reflect further on life and death, on love and belief. Her faith provided her with a perspective, which helped make her the woman she was. Because she had a perspective she helped to give others perspective too.

Sister Thomasine Cusack was a woman of prayer, a woman of learning, a woman of enthusiasm. She prayed with intensity and intelligence, with vigor and verve. Prayer was as natural and necessary to her as walking. Indeed, she had some prayers that she called her "outdoor prayers." These she would say as she walked, with dignity and style, the paths of the campus she loved so well.

One reason that prayer to her was very natural was because she did not separate God from her daily affairs. She chatted easily of God and to God—and never in clichés. Her intimacy with God had a contagion so that those with her often found it easier to turn to Him. There were certain things she liked to cite: God's mystical sense of humor, and sometimes the remark of Dame Alice, the wife of Sir Thomas More, "God is strangely silent."

Sister Thomasine was a woman of learning. She had long represented what is best in a teacher at a college such as Rosary, a combination of professional competence in her subject and a genuine concern for her students.

Sister Thomasine was a woman of enthusiasm. Because her enthusiasm was so carefully interwoven with love and kindness it was impossible for anyone to spend even the briefest time with her and not feel buoyed up—and able to do all the brave, good things she expected. It was even impossible to receive a hello from Sister Thomasine without having a feeling of being renewed. Because she had a perspective, she helped to give others perspective too. A student said to me after her death, "When she talked to you, she made you feel that God loved you and would care for you, and that everything would be all right." That's perspective. The Catholic Church helped Sister Thomasine to gain it, and it has helped me.

6. For Me, Christ Is Central

To me, Christ is central. This is the most telling reason why I am still a Catholic. Yet I find it the most difficult to write about. No doubt this is because it is the most personal —and the most private.

At different times in my life Christ has meant different things to me. At an early age the Infant Christ held appeal, and when I was a little older, the Christ who wanted little children to be allowed to come to Him. Later particular incidents or encounters with particular people had meaning. The miracle at Cana. The money-changers. The Samaritan woman. The Sermon on the Mount. And sadly—Christ weeping over Jerusalem.

Places too have played a part. When I visited Israel it was not Bethlehem and Nazareth that moved me. It was the Sea of Galilee, shining and clear. And the crowded, narrow streets of the Old City of Jerusalem. These to me were not only real, but were as they had been when Christ sailed and walked upon them. His presence could be felt.

By now, concepts for which Christ stood have assumed significance: compassion, concern for the suffering, a desire for justice, a love for all. His two great commandments, "You must love the Lord your God with all your heart, with all your soul, and with all your mind," and, "You must love your neighbor as yourself," encapsulate the only philosophy one needs, whatever one's role.

I should not have said it was difficult for me to write why

Christ is central in my life; I should have said it was impossible. I know I have done no more than indicate the place He holds for me. So much has been written about Him through the centuries, and yet nothing has been written. I can understand why. One does not describe the indescribable, nor fathom the unfathomable. I shall not try.

As I examine the different meanings Christ has held for me, overriding all is the sheer drama of His life. "This was no ordinary man." It is not surprising that *Godspell* continues to cast its spell on young people, nor that Burl Ives singing "Mary, Don't You Weep," or Marian Anderson singing "Were You There When They Crucified My Lord?" has an eloquence unmatched by sermons. (I suppose that after the reading of Scripture and books like François Mauriac's *Life of Jesus*, sermons should be one of the best ways to learn about Christ, but it is not always so. Perhaps Ronald Knox's brother, Wilfred, knew why this was not so. His niece Penelope Fitzgerald wrote, "He believed that a sermon should never last more than ten minutes; every minute after that bored the listener and undid the work of two minutes, so that after fifteen minutes you were, so to speak, preaching in reverse. . . .")

Those then are my reasons why I am still a Catholic. For many, not knowing where else to turn is a legitimate reason for remaining a Catholic. St. Peter himself asked Christ, "Lord, to whom shall we go?" It is not, however, a reason that appeals to me personally. For me, a more positive affirmation is that I am still a Catholic because I choose to be, not because there is no other place to go.

If, on the other hand, push came to shove, I too might ask, "Where would I turn?"

ON BEING A CATHOLIC

Richard P. McBrien

Past president of the Catholic Theological Society of America and recipient of its John Courtney Murray Award in 1976, Father McBrien is a priest of the Hartford, Connecticut, diocese, has served as a parish assistant and college chaplain, and obtained his doctorate in theology from the Gregorian University in Rome. He has taught at several colleges throughout the United States, was a visiting fellow in the John F. Kennedy School of Government at Harvard in 1975–76, and is presently professor of theology at Boston College, director of Boston College's Institute of Religious Education and Pastoral Ministry and a member of the board of trustees of the Boston Theological Institute. He has had articles appear in numerous publications and writes a weekly theological column syndicated in the Catholic Press for which he won awards from the Catholic Press Association in 1974, 1975, and 1978 for the best column in its field. He is the author of eleven books, among them *What Do We Really Believe?*, *Do We Need the Church?*, *Who Is a Catholic?*, and *The Remaking of the Church*.

I am a Catholic for many reasons, which can be grouped under two general headings: personal/biographical and theological/spiritual. The first two parts of this essay will identify and explain each reason within both these categories. These sections will deal, as objectively as possible, with "what *is*." The third part will offer exercises in alternation, and will deal with "what *if*." What *if* the personal/biographical data were different? What *if* the theological/spiritual interpretations and perspective were other than they are? Would I still be a Catholic?

1. *Personal/Biographical Reasons*

I am a Catholic, first, because I was born a Catholic. I do not suggest that the connection is at once inexorable and lasting. On the contrary, we American Catholics have been made painfully aware in recent decades that the "road to Damascus" is a two-way street. For many of our fellow citizens, particularly those in the entertainment business or in certain intellectual circles (the distinction is not always clear), the severing of one's Catholic roots somewhere in young adulthood is a matter of easy, almost casual, and sometimes bitter, public conversation.

On the other hand, being born and baptized a Catholic is a sociological given whose impact and abiding influence cannot readily be exaggerated. Taking the most standard statistics available, such as are published each year in *The Catholic Directory*, it is unmistakably the case that the overwhelming majority of Catholics enter the Church through infant baptism rather than through postadolescent conversion. I, for one, will not underestimate the significance of that primary biographical fact: I am a Catholic because I was born a Catholic. But that is not the only reason nor, for me today, the most important reason.

Many infants are baptized as Catholics, but not all are raised in a Catholic family environment. Indeed, there are nominal Catholics who look upon baptism or "christening" as a cherished family and cultural tradition, much like getting married in, or buried from, a church. I am a Catholic then, secondly, because I was also nurtured as a Catholic in a Catholic home by Catholic parents. This is not to say that the atmosphere was overbearingly Catholic; it was not. But Catholicism was taken seriously, honored always if sometimes in the breach. If what the psychologists tell us about our formative years is true, then Catholicism is deep within my psychic fiber.

I am a Catholic, thirdly, because of environmental influences beyond the family. I was, from the beginning, sustained by an interlocking network of Catholic relationships, both personal and institutional. Most relatives, friends, and neighbors participated in this same theological, spiritual, and cultural universe known as Roman Catholicism. But even in my youngest years the doctrine of Leonard Feeney ("outside the Catholic Church, no salvation") had no real hold within that network. Ecumenism was a natural style long before the Second Vatican Council formally endorsed it. Our neighborhood was mixed—religiously, denominationally, ethnically, and, to a minimal extent, racially. Friendships bore the same pluralistic character. And yet Catholicism was a strong, almost taken-for-granted value among those who professed it.

There were institutional supports as well, particularly the parish and the school. I was an altar boy as soon as I was old enough to qualify for liturgical service, and although kindergarten and the first six grades were spent in the local public school, I attended Catholic junior high and a seminary high school. And during those early years in public grammar school, I was faithful to weekly catechism classes taught by the parish nuns.

These personal and institutional affiliations with the Catholic faith were accentuated and deepened by my lifelong vocational interest in, and pursuit of, the priesthood. I wanted to be a priest for as long as I can remember, even though, from time to time, I thought the priesthood could legitimately be combined with, or temporarily set aside for, other professional interests, ranging from baseball to politics. I know that today I would not be a theologian if I had not decided to study for the priesthood. I am confident that I would still be a Catholic, however. But that is a question for the third section of this piece.

In any case, one cannot overestimate the extent and intensity of theological formation one receives throughout a twelve-year seminary program. Our religion courses frequently lapsed into indoctrination, but on occasion they were intellectually provocative and engaging. A growing passion for American political history would eventually converge with more serious theological inquiries into the Catholic Church's social teachings. That social doctrine would prove to be, as it remains even now, one of the strongest positive reasons for my remaining a Catholic.

Catholicism's hold on me has been strengthened by the subsequent and continuing exercise of that vocational pursuit. I served for a year and a half as a parish priest, a year concurrent with that as a part-time college chaplain, two years as a graduate student at pontifical university in Rome, five years as a major seminary professor of theology, four more years on a part-time basis (nine years in all in seminary residence), more than twelve years (at this writing) as a weekly syndicated theology columnist in the Catholic press, about the same length of time (and still going strong) as a lecturer in all parts of the United States, Canada, and other countries, as a consultant to dioceses, religious congregations of women and men alike, and various national organizations, as an author of eleven books on the Church and related topics, as a professor of theology in a Catholic university, and as director of a religious education and pastoral ministry institute at the same university.

If Catholicism was in my psychic fiber from my earliest years, it has been pumping vigorously through my social and intellectual arteries ever since. But these are what I have called personal and biographical reasons for my commitment to Catholic faith. Since I am by profession a theologian, the reader may find my theological reasons at once more interesting and more significant.

2. Theological/Spiritual Reasons

Without denying the shaping influence of those psychological, sociological, cultural, and even geographical factors over which I have had no immediate control, not to say totally conscious awareness, I should insist that I am a Catholic by conviction rather than by habit alone. I am a Catholic because I am a Christian, because I am persuaded by the distinctive claims of Roman Catholicism within the Body of Christ, because I am impressed by the broad horizon against which the Roman Catholic tradition confronts specific issues, because of Roman Catholicism's attentiveness to the rational, the voluntary, and the aesthetic, because of its corresponding attentiveness to history and continuity within history, because of its drive toward, and capacity for, systematization, because of the impact this whole complex of attitudes has upon specific questions and problems which I must face as a theologian and upon those elements which frame and form my existence as a Christian, and because, finally, of the incarnation of the Roman Catholic ideal in others, past and present, whom I respect for their humanity and for their Christian integrity. I shall explain each of these reasons in sequence.

One is a Christian before one is a Catholic. To ask why one is a Catholic without asking beforehand why one is a Christian misses the fundamental connection between Catholicism and Christian faith. "Catholic" modifies "Christian," not vice versa. To a Christian means, before all else, that one accepts Jesus of Nazareth as the Christ. Jesus does not simply participate in the universal christhood still in cosmic process. Jesus *is* the Christ.

St. John's Gospel makes clear, for example, that "the Word became flesh and dwelt among us, full of grace and truth" and that all this "grace and truth came through Jesus Christ" (1:14, 17). When John the Baptist was asked directly if he were the Christ, he replied straightforwardly, "I am not the Christ" (John 1:20). If there were anything substantive to this separation of the historical Jesus from the universal Christ, then surely a man so close to God as John the Baptist would have shared in this christic reality. The identification of the Jesus of history with the universal Christ is similarly clear in the early Church's preaching: "This Jesus, whom I proclaim to you, is the Christ," Paul declared (Acts 17:3). Other texts of this sort abound throughout the New Testament. One needs only the time and patience to work his or her way through a good biblical concordance.

I cannot provide here a full apologetical argument for the Lordship of Jesus, but the passage of fifteen years has not detracted, in my mind at least, from the persuasiveness of an argument formulated by Avery Dulles, S.J., in his *Apologetics and the Biblical Christ*. The portrait of Jesus which emerges from the New Testament is one that simply "rings true," as Dulles puts it:

> If men of the first century, whether Jews or Gentiles, had been asked to conjecture in what form God might appear on earth, none would have imagined Him coming in such a guise, so humble, gentle, and utterly human. . . . He constantly does the most unexpected things, revolutionizing the accepted norms of conduct. He praises pagans and prostitutes, draws near to Samaritans and lepers. He attacks the most respected classes, and insults His hosts at dinner. In the midst of His intense labors He finds time to welcome little children to Himself. He rebukes the wind and the waves, but falls silent before His accusers. Men would never have fabri-

cated such a figure as their religious leader, and precisely for this reason the Gospels have undying power to convert human hearts. [P. 39.]

Hans Küng's recently formulated argument on behalf of Jesus Christ in *On Being a Christian* is more comprehensive, if also wordier. The ambitiousness of Küng's project notwithstanding, he can do no more than demonstrate the reasonableness, not the ultimate rationality, of Christian faith:

> This sustaining reality of God is never granted to me intuitively, unequivocally, free of doubt, securely. . . . The believer, like the lover, has no conclusive proofs to give him complete security. But the believer too, like the lover, can be completely certain of the Other by committing himself entirely to the Other. And this certainty is stronger than all the security established by proofs. [P. 163.]

I am a Catholic, secondly, because I am persuaded by the distinctive Roman Catholic claim that it is the one church within the Body of Christ which retains, in principle, all of the constitutive elements willed directly or indirectly by the Lord himself: Sacred Scripture, doctrines, sacraments, and ministries, including the Petrine office. The qualification, "in principle," is an important one because I am not saying that the Catholic Church alone, or even to the highest degree, is faithful to the mind and heart of Christ and to the core of his gospel. I am arguing, rather, that there are elements which belong essentially to the Christian community, without which that community would not be the Church, and that none of these essential elements is rejected by Roman Catholicism nor is institutionally absent from Catholicism's life, order, and mission. On the contrary, the Catholic Church affirms them all and insists upon their presence for the sake of the integrity of the Body of Christ.

I am sympathetic, therefore, with Charles Davis's argument in *A Question of Conscience* that there is indeed a distinctively Roman Catholic claim about itself and that this has to do with its structures. He defines the latter as the "ordered systems of social relationships, institutions that embody these relationships, the self-understanding of the structured community as formulated in its public, official documents, and the attitudes and actions that result from the structured relationships, institutions, doctrines and laws" (p. 58). At the heart of this structural network is the Petrine ministry. The Roman Catholic Church teaches that the pope is the successor of Peter as bishop of Rome and, as such, possesses a primacy of jurisdiction over the whole Church. This doctrine was formally declared by the First Vatican Council in 1870 and was reaffirmed almost a century later by the Second Vatican Council in the third chapter of its *Dogmatic Constitution on the Church.*

Davis assumes, however, that official Roman Catholic teaching on the papacy is incompatible with any model of government other than the monarchical, and an absolutely monarchical form at that. The work of the Canon Law Society of America in the years since Davis separated himself from the Roman Catholic Church is indicative of the kind of theological and canonical flexibility there is in that fundamental teaching. I have tried in a work of my own, *The Remaking of the Church: An Agenda for Reform*, to recapitulate the substance of these various studies and to provide an ecclesiological interpretation of recent institutional developments and crises within the Catholic Church. The present essay can do no more than offer a sketch or outline of my reasons for being and remaining a Catholic. My *Remaking of the Church*, as well as my *Who Is a Catholic?*, *Roman Catholicism*, and my contribution to the *Infallibility Debate* collection, provide a much fuller statement of my theological position regarding such delicate issues as papal infallibility, the limitation of papal authority, papal elections, the constitutional implications of collegiality, and so forth.

Recent ecumenical consultations, particularly the Lutheran–Roman Catholic dialogue, have reinforced rather than weakened my conviction that the Petrine office is constitutive to the Church. The Lutheran–Roman Catholic common statement on the papacy in 1974 acknowledges that the Church universal requires a specific ministry which attends to the needs of the Church as a whole: "to promote or preserve the oneness of the church by symbolizing unity, and by facilitating communication, mutual assistance or correction, and collaboration in the church's mission. . . . the single most notable representative of this Ministry toward the church universal, both in duration and geographical scope, has been the bishop of Rome."

But this remains, of course, *the* ecumenical issue, which Hans Küng heralded as such on the eve of Vatican II in his *The Council, Reform and Reunion:* "The chief difficulty in the way of reunion lies in the two different concepts of the Church, and especially of the concrete organizational structure of the Church. . . . Ultimately, all questions about the concrete organizational structure of the Church are crystallized in the question of *ecclesiastical office*" (pp. 128–29). It is the one issue which finally divides the Catholic from all other Christian churches, various other differences regarding liturgy, spirituality, theology, polity, and doctrinal formulations notwithstanding. When all else is stripped away, the official Catholic position on the Petrine ministry is different from every other official and/or representative position of every other formal Christian church. This is not to suggest that it must always be so. On the contrary, the Lutheran–Roman Catholic consultation gives promise of some future breakthrough. But for the time being at least, the papacy question is the question that finally sets Catholic ecclesiology off from all others. As a theologian and as an ecclesiologist, I do not see how the question of Catholic identity can be answered without reference to the Petrine ministry or to one's personal attitude toward it.

I am impressed, thirdly, with the broad horizon against which Roman Catholicism confronts and interprets reality. That mode of interpretation is balanced, dialectically sensitive, and *catholic*. The dialectic which operates in Catholic theology emerges from the polarities of human existence itself. "The effect of this dialectic throughout the history of theology," John Macquarrie writes in *Principles of Christian Theology*, "has been to exclude extreme and exaggerated points of view. The Church needs both stability and flexibility in its theology if it is to go forward, and not be either disintegrated or petrified" (p. vi). No theologian more effectively maintains this sense of dialectical balance and catholicity than Karl Rahner, S.J., who, Macquarrie freely admits, "handles in a masterly way those tensions which constitute the peculiar dialectic of theology mentioned above: faith and reason, tradition and novelty, authority and freedom, and so on" (p. vii).

Nowhere is this balance more carefully preserved than in the theology of the Catholic Church's most important thinker, Thomas Aquinas. He does not choose *between* reason and faith: theology is a work of reason illumined by faith. He does not choose *between* nature and grace; grace builds on nature and presupposes it. The philosophy of Aquinas is essentially realistic and concrete. It does not begin with some abstract notion from which reality is to be deduced but starts from the existing world and inquires about its being: the what, the how, the conditions. In this sense Thomas's philosophy is existentialist, although Aquinas himself could not be called an existentialist in the modern meaning of the word. He constructed his philosophy by reflection on sense-experience, and there is a commendable objectivity to his arguments.

On the other hand, God is the last end of all our knowledge of reality. Indeed, God is the very plenitude of Being, *ipsum esse subsistens*. Without the grace of revelation, we cannot come to that fullness of knowledge which has God as its final object. Accordingly, God remains the ultimate horizon for all of our insights, acts of understanding, our judgments, and our decisions. No horizon is broader than this, and yet since God remains elusive this side of the Kingdom (John 1:18), our probings into reality are always tempered by that consciousness of our own finitude and the inherent limitations of our inquiry after truth.

I am impressed, fourthly, with Catholicism's attentiveness

to the rational, the voluntary, and the aesthetic, without pitting one over against the other two or without suppressing one or another component of human experience and expression. Baptist theologian Langdon Gilkey has correctly linked this catholicity of experience and expression with Catholicism's historic regard for symbolism. More than any other religious tradition perhaps, Catholicism has insisted upon the essentially sacramental character of reality and of God's encounter with us and ours with God. Edward Schillebeeckx's influential book on the sacraments, *Christ the Sacrament of Encounter with God*, is only one of many indications of this emphasis in Catholic thought, and it is not at all surprising that Avery Dulles's *Models of the Church* should have focused so sharply on the sacramental character of Church as the most distinctively Catholic model. Symbols, Gilkey suggests, can be "sensuous, aesthetic, and celebratory as well as verbal and intellectual." He continues:

> It is strange but understandable that a sacramental and so symbolic mode of religiosity may possess more creative possibilities within modernity than either the classical Protestant emphasis on the sacred Word alone or the spiritualistic Protestant (and now pentecostal) emphasis on a transrational presence of the Spirit. For a symbol combines, without destroying either one, absoluteness and relativity better than either propositional dogmas or verbal proclamation. The symbol points to and communicates a divinity that lies beyond it. . . . Furthermore, the experience of the symbol can unite sensual, aesthetic, and intellectual experience more readily than the experiences of proclamation or of an ecstatic spiritual presence. (Pp. 21–22.)

For Gilkey, Catholicism may provide "the best entrance" into a new synthesis of the Christian tradition for which the modern age calls. The success of the project, however, will depend upon Catholicism's "creative ability to separate the sacramental principle from the objectivist, absolutist, and anachronistic embodiments in which it was imprisoned and recently made ineffective, and to reinterpret and re-embody that principle in *contemporary* terms" (p. 22).

The same challenge, of course, faces the Catholic Church in its handling of the three major components of this new synthesis: the rational, the voluntary, and the aesthetic. Can it effectively separate its "drive toward rationality" (to use Gilkey's phrase) from its occasional lapses into rationalism on the one extreme, manifested in the apologetics textbooks and techniques of the early twentieth century, and into an unquestioning embrace of both philosophical and doctrinal traditions on the other extreme, manifested in the extraordinary durability of decadent Scholasticism and of dogmatic fundamentalism. "One might say," Gilkey suggests, "that in traditional Catholic life the speculative but not the critical powers of reason were accepted" (p. 23).

Catholicism's regard for the voluntary and the aesthetic is similarly mixed. Its "remarkable sense of humanity and grace . . . the love of life, the appreciation of the body and the senses, of joy and celebration, the tolerance of the sinner, these natural, worldly and 'human' virtues are far more clearly and universally embodied in Catholics and in Catholic life than in Protestants and in Protestantism" (pp. 17–18). And yet a whole new generation of explicit ex-Catholics (the Phil Donahues of television, the Mary McCarthys of literature, the Kareem Abdul-Jabbars of sport) bemoans Catholicism's moralistic hammerlock on the psyche, the Jansenism of its sexual ethic, the pervasive fear of hell, the rejection of pleasure, the oppressiveness and insensitivity of its authority figures.

I am a Catholic still because I perceive these admixtures of rationality and rationalism and of morality and moralism as inconsistent with, not constitutive of, the Roman Catholic tradition. The Church's deliberate and critically self-conscious move away from rationalism and moralism in recent years does not represent a compromise with modernity but a recovery of that tradition, as the works of Schillebeeckx, Rahner, Bernard Haring, Yves Congar, Bernard Lonergan, and others convincingly show.

I am impressed, fifthly, with Catholicism's regard for history. The Roman Catholic Church is certainly not the only church which presumes to trace its roots back to the New Testament period itself, but since the matter of origin is an essential ecclesiological question for Catholicism, it is committed by that very fact to a particular attentiveness to history and to continuity within history. It is not enough for Catholicism to assert that it has its source in Christ and the apostolic community; it must also demonstrate its abiding fidelity to his and their word, witness, and service. Apostolicity is a mark of the Church, i.e., a characteristic without which the Church would not be the Church.

It is not a question here of arguing that the Catholic Church is better than all of the other Christian churches on this point or on any of the others, but only that there is within Roman Catholicism a configuration of values (rationality, aestheticism, respect for history and continuity, etc.) which one does not readily discover elsewhere or which, in any case, commend Catholicism on its own merits, without regard for competing configurations. It would, therefore, be unfair to suggest, and difficult to prove in any case, that Roman Catholicism is more faithful to history and more clearly continuous with the New Testament Church itself than any other Christian body. But ecumenical propriety does not prevent my saying that no other Christian church *better* serves history and continuity.

The work of Karl Rahner and, before him, of John Henry Newman and, before him, of Thomas Aquinas and, before him, of Augustine exposes the historical genius of Roman Catholicism in a way that is, by all serious accounts, classic. Rahner is an especially useful example because he is our contemporary. No one can skim through, much less carefully examine, his multivolume *Theological Investigations* or his many independent monographs without recognizing a constant attentiveness to history and continuity. He approaches present-day theological questions according to a method that, far from dispensing with the past, moves the tradition forward in new and critically constructive ways. His recent

Foundations of Christian Faith is an excellent case in point; and in particular its treatment of the Catholic Church's legitimacy as the Church of Christ, an issue that is at once delicate and sensitive:

> Hence we can propose in a formal way as the first principle that an ecclesial institution can be regarded as an institution to which we can entrust ourselves as the church of Christ if and to the extent that it has the most concrete historical continuity possible with the church of original Christianity. We cannot simply leap over the ages in between and reject them as anti-Christian, antichurch, and anti-Christ. For otherwise we would have done away with this incarnational, historical and corporeal continuity, and hence also with a corporeal and ecclesial reality which is independent of us. [P. 354.]

There is in Catholicism, as Langdon Gilkey insists, "a sense of the reality, importance, and 'weight' of tradition and history in the formation of this people and so of her religious truths, religious experience, and human wisdom" (p. 17). To be sure, reverence for history and tradition can degenerate into traditionalism, and has. But the aberration is not inevitably implied in the substance. Indeed, as Rahner's own work shows, Catholicism is entirely capable of exploiting the one without lapsing into the other.

Catholicism commends itself to me, sixthly, because of its capacity for systematization, for seeing or attempting to see all of reality as a piece, in all of its interrelationships. One might call it Catholicism's capacity for architectonic vision.

Surely, Catholicism has not been alone in producing great works of systematic theology, but with Thomas Aquinas it has at least set a standard for the rest. Our legitimate criticisms of the so-called Catholic manual theology of the early twentieth century notwithstanding, it had the virtue of trying to imitate the best, of trying to discover and underscore the intrinsic order and coherence of the Christian message.

The work of Bernard Lonergan, although, in my judgment, less formally theological than Karl Rahner's, confirms and accentuates this Catholic bias in favor of systematization. Lonergan's project is undertaken not so much at the theological level as at the philosophical—i.e., at the level at which the fundamental operations of the human mind are engaged: experiencing, understanding, judging, and deciding. There is a unity and a relatedness to these operations which exist and function before we manage to advert to them explicitly, understand them, or objectify them. Transcendental method, according to Lonergan, brings to light these conscious operations of the mind and leads to the answers to three basic questions: What am I doing when I am knowing? Why is doing that knowing? What do I know when I do it? "The first answer is a cognitional theory," Lonergan writes in *Method in Theology*. "The second is an epistemology. The third is a metaphysics where, however, the metaphysics is transcendental, an *integration* of heuristic structures, and not some categorical speculation that reveals that all is water, or matter, or spirit, or process, or what have you" (p. 25, italics mine).

I am a Catholic, seventhly, because of the impact the preceding four factors have upon specific questions which confront me as a theologian—e.g., Christ, Church, the relationship between nature and grace, Kingdom of God, etc.—as well as upon those elements which frame and form my existence as a Christian—e.g., the Eucharist.

If I were not a Catholic, it is likely that my Christology would be more adoptionist than classical, for, apart from history and doctrinal tradition, my theological instincts would be more reductionist than conservative. I am conservative in my Christology—i.e., I insist as strongly on the divine as on the human character of Jesus Christ—not because I am conservative by disposition but because of my sense of intellectual responsibility to the Catholic tradition.

If I were not Catholic, I might be tempted to view the Church less as a mystery and more as an agent of social change. But because I am a Catholic, with Catholicism's distinctively sacramental perspective, I view the Church as a reality at once spiritual and institutional. My sense of urgency about ecclesiastical reform is as much a function of my conviction that the Church is a sacrament of Christ and must communicate what it embodies as it is a function of my politically liberal commitment to due process, the limitation of power, accountability, constitutionalism, and the like.

If I were not Catholic, I might stress the prerogatives of nature at the expense of grace—i.e., I would more likely be liberal than something closer to neo-orthodox (to use David Tracy's models). That failure to keep nature and grace in proper dialectical balance would similarly disrupt my perception of the relationship between the divine and the human in the coming of the Kingdom of God. Walter Rauschenbusch, James Luther Adams, and others in the liberal Protestant tradition would appeal seductively to my liberal political philosophy, and I might find myself less critical of Latin American liberation theology than I am, or of some of the easy identifications of certain public causes with God's own cause. The Kingdom is the product neither of human effort, nor of divine initiative alone. The former is, in fact, "of vital concern" to the latter, according to the Second Vatican Council's *Pastoral Constitution on the Church in the Modern World,* § 39. There is a commendable balance in the conciliar teaching and it is reflected as well in such contemporary Catholic theologians as Rahner, Schillebeeckx, Johannes Metz, Hans Küng, and others. Indeed, I have tried to formulate such an eschatological position in one of my earlier books, *Church: The Continuing Quest.*

If I were not Catholic, finally, I should probably not even begin to worship God and celebrate the wonders of redemption in any sustained and sustaining way. The Eucharist is, for me, the right response to the call to worship. The language, the ritual, the interaction of persons and symbols, the intersection of past, present, and future, the sense of community, however modest it might be—all these are such that I could find no greater or more compelling liturgical sustenance than I continue to discover in the ritual breaking of the bread and sharing of the cup.

I am a Catholic, eighthly, because of the incarnation of

Roman Catholic, and ultimately of Christian and human, values in those others—family, friends, acquaintances, colleagues, major political figures inside and outside the ecclesiastical organization—who share or have shared the Roman Catholic tradition with me. Again it is the Catholic sacramental principle at work. This eighth reason has to do as well with that whole network of personal relationships which the Catholic Church calls the communion of saints and which not even death and purgation can obliterate. Not coincidentally, belief in the communion of saints is creedally linked with belief in the forgiveness of sins. Even in its darkest theological and pastoral hours, when it seemed to do its worst to confuse and torment its most vulnerable members, the Catholic Church had always preached the enduring message of Jesus that no sin but that against the Holy Spirit is beyond forgiveness.

As one reviews these reasons for being and remaining a Catholic, the personal/biographical on the one hand and the theological/spiritual on the other, one might reasonably ask whether one set of reasons is determinative of the other. Would the theological/spiritual reasons be unthinkable were it not for the personal/biographical? Clearly, that cannot be the case as a matter of necessity, since there are thousands of our contemporaries, not to mention the thousands who preceded them, who entered the Catholic Church as adults, after a conversion experience of one kind or another. And yet the question is a fair and valid one. How many Catholics, this writer included, would be Catholic were it not for the accidents of birth and family upbringing?

Conversely, to what extent do the theological/spiritual factors impinge upon, and profoundly influence, our subsequent personal/biographical development? I should prefer to prescind from the which-came-first-the-chicken-or-the-egg dilemma and suggest instead, in characteristically Catholic fashion, that the influence is less chronological than dialectical, and that, in any case, the more conscious we are of the so-called determinative factors, the less determinative those factors are upon our experiencing, our understanding, our judging, and our deciding. I am satisfied that I have not achieved a condition of pure objectivity, but I am also satisfied that I cherish objectivity as a value and as a goal, and that I am open in principle to disengage myself from all subjective and socially institutional forces which can and do distort one's architectonic vision of reality.

3. Exercises in Alternation

No Christian has the task and the obligation because he is a Christian to step out of the historical situation of his existence, and to want to ground the concreteness of his existence exclusively by means of reflection. Such a thing is impossible a priori both for human knowledge and for the actualization of human existence, and hence it cannot be required here. This of course does not deny a person's obligation to reflect responsibly upon his own situation, to place it in question in a certain sense, and perhaps in certain circumstances, because of his existential experience of life and his reflection upon it, even to alter very radically the situation in which he finds himself.

Karl Rahner's observation in *Foundations of Christian Faith* (pp. 350–51) provides a contextual qualification of what follows here. I can ask, for the sake of speculation, what might have happened had life's circumstances been different, but in the end I have to accept the facticity of existence and, theologically, its ultimate grounding in the will of God. The historical facts of Christian disunity or even of religious pluralism do not stem, in the main, from personal guilt. They are to be placed in an immediate and intensive sense "on God's account," where they have and must have, a positive meaning of salvific providence.

If I had been born a Protestant, it is more than likely that I should still be a Protestant, just as Martin Marty, George Lindbeck, James Gustafson, and other Protestant theologians I admire and respect remain faithful to their particular traditions. Given my intellectual disposition, however, it is un-likely that I should have remained satisfied with a Protestant tradition very far removed from what I should call the main-stream of Protestant experience and theology: Episcopalian, Lutheran, Presbyterian, and the like. Had I been born a Jew, I should probably still be a Jew, lodged theologically some-where between Reform and Conservative; had I been born Orthodox, I should by now have moved toward Reform Juda-ism. Had I been born a Moslem or within some other non-Christian, non-Jewish religion, I have no clue at all to what I'd be today, so culturally foreign are those religious tradi-tions. Had I, finally, been born without any religion at all, it is entirely plausible that I would still be a humanist without denominational attachment or I might by now have edged at least into some form of liberal Protestantism. Speculation of this sort does little more perhaps than tantalize. The "what ifs" are all moot in any case. But collectively they do under-line the crucial significance of the personal and the bio-graphical for the making of religious self-definitions.

If I were not sustained personally, environmentally, institu-tionally, or vocationally as a Catholic, would I remain a Catholic? Again, I don't know. I do know that I am capable of changing my opinions and, once in a great while, even some deeply rooted convictions as time and circumstances have progressed. My views on the Church, on salvation, on specific questions of morality, on God—all are different now from what they were ten, fifteen, or twenty years ago. That I am capable of change is reasonably clear. How much change I am radically open to, and whether I am really open in prin-ciple to a change from Catholicism to some other form of Christianity or indeed to something apart from Christianity, is but another unanswerable question. I am reassured by the fact that I raise it and by the fact that I acknowledge its am-biguity. It means, or at least suggests, that change is not to-tally foreclosed by rigidity of mind and spirit.

Obviously, if I were to lose hold of Jesus Christ, I could no longer remain a Christian, much less a Catholic. Is that a possibility? The only reasonable answer is that it *is* a possi-

bility. A probability, then? No, the present current of christo-
logical reductionism even within some Roman Catholic theological circles notwithstanding. I am not at all sympathetic
with it and would more likely reject faith in the Lordship of
Jesus outright than try and maintain a faint Christian heart-
beat through some liberal arterial bypass.

Would it be possible or probable, on the other hand, that
I should maintain faith in Jesus Christ and feel compelled
nonetheless to separate myself from the Roman Catholic
Church? Yes, it is possible; no, it is not probable. I should
suspect, however ironic it may seem, that losing faith in Jesus
Christ would occur before a loss of faith in Catholicism's distinctive claims, if indeed either were to occur at all. It is, of
course, conceivable that a pope may someday define, as a
matter of dogmatic belief, a teaching which is wholly incompatible with that architectonic vision to which I have previously referred. There would be a period of intense argument, confrontation, and regrouping among the Church's
theologians much like the period immediately following the
publication of *Humanae Vitae* in 1968, and I would be very
attentive, if not always responsive, to the judgments of some
of my more distinguished colleagues. But what is conceivable
is not probable. What is perhaps probable is a breach opened
not by dogmatic pronouncement but by disciplinary fiat. It is
neither unthinkable nor improbable, because in fact it has
happened, that an ecclesiastical authority should employ certain canonical pressures in the interests of theological "orthodoxy." A priest-theologian marries. A dispensation is refused.
A professional position, subject to attack. The relationship
with the Catholic community is compromised and the possibility of eventual severance heightened. The route taken by
Charles Davis, on the other hand, is far less probable;
namely, a negatively critical reexamination of traditional
Roman Catholic claims regarding the hierarchical structure
of the Church and, in particular, the primacy of the Petrine
office.

I am convinced, although personal conviction alone is no
guarantee of immunity from error, that I could never lose

hold of those characteristically Catholic values to which I have already referred—namely, dialectically balanced thinking, attentiveness to the rational, the voluntary, and the aesthetic, regard for history and continuity, and the drive toward systematization. Those values reflect my own fundamental philosophical perspective on reality and are not finally dependent upon my commitment to Catholicism as such. On the other hand, these two commitments—to those philosophical values, and to the Church which historically has embodied and promoted them—are mutually supportive and sustaining, one of the other.

I wonder most, perhaps, about the effect of widespread defections of respected Catholic colleagues from the Church, not simply from the priesthood or organized religious communities. We Catholics have made much of John Henry Newman's entry into the Church. What would we, or I, make of the departure of Karl Rahner, Hans Küng, Avery Dulles, Cardinal Leo Suenens, Archbishop Helder Camara, Mother Teresa, Dorothy Day, John Tracy Ellis, Theodore Hesburgh, David Tracy, or any number of other close friends whose names would not elicit instant recognition but whose impact upon my life has been considerable? I suspect that their decision to reject Catholicism would challenge my present ecclesiastical affiliation far more dramatically and in a far more penetrating manner than theological controversy, canonical pressure, or spiritual transformation. If their present commitment to, and incarnation of, Catholic, Christian, and human values is one of the most powerful forces sustaining my relationship with the Catholic Church, their exodus from that Church would have a most sobering effect, to say the least, on my own ecclesiological vision. It seems to me that one simply cannot overestimate the influence, for good or for ill, of one's closest associates. That can be taken as a cynically deterministic observation or one that fortifies the historic Catholic belief in the centrality of the sacramental principle. I prefer the latter interpretation.

I am a Roman Catholic, therefore, by experience and by

conviction. Could the dialectical connection between the two ever collapse or be disrupted? Yes, and under the kind of circumstances alluded to in the preceding exercises in alternation. But that connection is still present and operative, and I make no apologies for it. When I feel I must begin to apologize for it, I will know that either the experiential or the theological pole has given way. I will make it my business at that point to find out which, and to what extent. And I shall always be prepared, I should hope, to face the possibility that alternation may have to be more than an exercise. For the many reasons set forth in this essay, I am not at all close to that point.

WHY I AM A CATHOLIC

ABIGAIL McCARTHY

Author, lecturer, educator, and mother of four, Abigail McCarthy has been a teacher in secondary public schools and a college professor, and lectures all over the United States. She is founding president of the Clearinghouse on Women's Issues, an association of major women's organizations in the United States, and active in numerous women's organizations. She was United States delegate to the 1974 Berlin Conference, is a director of the Dreyfus Corporation and trustee of Trinity College and College of St. Catherine, is a member of Phi Beta Kappa and Pi Lambda Theta, and is the recipient of five honorary doctorates. She has contributed articles to numerous magazines and newspapers, among them the New York *Times*, *The Atlantic Monthly*, the *Washington Post*, and *The New Republic*, is a columnist for *One Woman's Voice*, has a regular column in *Commonweal*, and is the author of *Private Faces/Public Places* and *Circles*.

Why am I a Catholic? The question is usually posed to me a bit differently. Why, I am asked, are you *still* a Catholic? Much of my life is lived among people to whom that is a real question. For various reasons.

There are many people in our society who do not see any religion as part of what they think of as the real world. These range from those on the heights of our financial and political systems (although there *are*, certainly, believers in such places) to the everyday, hard-bitten service men who come to fix the washer or read the meter. Among the latter I have encountered those who are the very embodiment of cynicism, men incapable, it seems, of conceiving of disinterestedness or idealism anywhere, and yet they are good-natured and cheerful in their disbelief. The question, as it comes from them, unspoken but only implied in attitude, is oddly shaking.

There are those others who were born in the world of achievement, who have been rapidly upwardly mobile, and who, on the way, have left the largely *pro forma* religion of childhood behind. Among these are those who found their religion a business or social handicap. A good number are former Catholics who gibe, with what they fancy as great good humor, at old practices and old beliefs—things, they seem to say, one naturally leaves behind in the process of growth. The question from them is merely irritating. They are so blithe in their assumption of a lack of sophistication on the part of anyone still in the Church. They often display a complete and feckless ignorance of the changes in the Church and hold that I believe things I have never believed. They are forever telling old horror stories about their parochial school life —about the sister who warned the girls against wearing patent leather slippers, for example. To me these stories seem a kind of folklore; they are so often told, and so contrary to my experience.

More and more often now the question is asked me by women who share many of my own concerns. Coming from them it is a pained and painful question. Why indeed am I still a practicing member of a church in which every practice, custom, rite, and regulation seems to relegate me to less than a full share in humanity—except perhaps in the next world. But in this the Church seems only more explicit—and perhaps more honest in bias—than others among the institutions of my world. I suppose that if I were to abandon Catholicism because the juridical and legal Church puts me in a secondary place, I would have left long ago. I am, after all, a lay person and whatever I suffer in the Church as a woman, I suffered first as a lay person.

The question troubles me most when it comes from the embittered and the broken. They are often people who offered the Church talents, dedication, their youth, or their maturity and, when they unwittingly obstructed some official's way or when they roused controversy, were disposed of as casually as one would dispose of paper towels. In one of its aspects the Church is a rather moribund bureaucracy. How, ask these with considerable justice, can I continue to belong to an institution in which respect for the individual is of so little concern?

I am also troubled when the question comes from those aflame against injustice who see the Church in thrall to the powerful and the rich. But not only is this view, thus stated, far from the whole truth, but the reformer's zeal often has strange roots. It may stem from pity for the misery of the poor; it may stem from a desire to be a savior for the sake of being a savior. Of the one root Bernanos' crusty old Curé de Torcy warned (in *Diary of a Country Priest*) when he said, "Pity is powerful and devouring. . . . One of the strongest passions of man that's what it is." And he recognized the other in one of the world's reformers. "I'm certain he was madly thirsting for justice. But Almighty God doesn't like us to meddle with His justice and His wrath is rather too much for poor devils like us. It intoxicates. . . . Even though in essentials he was just, his ire had poisoned him by inches . . ." I have what I suppose is a healthy Catholic fear of image-breakers. Yet I do not deny the force of the question when it comes from those hungering and thirsting after justice. It demands an answer.

Why am I a Catholic? Surely because I choose to be. I do not fully understand my choice, but I am willing to look at my experience of the Church in search for that understanding.

Curiously enough, the question has never been raised by those of my own children who do not practice the faith. To them my being Catholic seems to be an integral part of my identity. Perhaps I should say of their mother's identity, since it is a rare child who thinks of a parent as a separate being. They are even a bit disturbed if I abandon a practice they associate with my *Catholicness*. Obviously to them I would be less than myself, not myself, if I were no longer Catholic. Being Catholic is a strand in the personality of the person I have become. It is part of others' perception of me as a person; it is part of my perception of myself. When I said as much to a rather irascible bishop of my acquaintance, he snorted impatiently, "Nonsense—that's the cultural argument. You stay in the Church because it has transmitted truth since the time of Christ and mediates grace to you through the sacraments."

Possibly, but the words are flat and fairly meaningless as a measure of my experience. Whence this certitude, if in fact I do have it? I was, in the popular way of expressing it, *born* into the Church as I was born into my family. Just as the Incarnation occurred at a particular time and place and the Son of God came forth from a people who had been lovingly prepared over a thousand years—may it not follow that there is a mysterious connection in the way I, and each one of us, became participants in this incarnation through other human beings, through a family, a people, a church? My ability to assent to incorporation into the Church has depended on my experience with it and in it, because it is, after all, a matter of choice, or, in the more churchly phrase, of my free will.

I must admit that quite possibly I would not be a Catholic if my early experience had been of the Church as an enemy of the intellect or of the creative impulse and beauty. So many people insist that they met with such enmity in childhood or early adolescence that I have to suppose that parochial life was—and still is—inimical to mind and creativity in many parts of the country. One could call it a grace that the Church of my youth was the ally of intelligence and excellence in learning, and affirmative of beauty in art and music. And my experience was not totally unusual. The brilliant and controversial author Mary McCarthy has written in her *Memories of a Catholic Girlhood*, "There was the Catholicism I learned from my mother and from the simple parish priest and nuns in Minneapolis, which was, on the whole, a religion of beauty and goodness, however imperfectly realized."

She writes, too, and many Catholics must feel a shock of recognition in reading it, "Our ugly church and parish school provided me with my only aesthetic outlet, in the words of the Mass and the litanies and the old Latin hymns, in the Easter lilies around the altar, rosaries, ornamented prayer books, votive lamps, holy cards stamped in gold and decorated with flower wreaths and a saint's picture. This side of Catholicism, much of it cheapened and debased by mass production, was for me, nevertheless, the equivalent of Gothic cathedrals and illuminated manuscripts and mystery plays."

Unlike the ugly, graceless atmosphere in which the orphaned Mary McCarthy was forced to live, where the people "had a positive gift for turning everything sour and ugly" and even religious books were banned, my childhood home, although threadbare, was one in which books, music, and art were valued, but I am sure that the ceaseless effort made in our small parish church—it seemed big to me then—to surround the things of God with beauty and ceremony had the same lasting effect on me. And, like her, I remember parochial school education as a system in which excellence was striven for and achievement rewarded.

It mattered, too, I think, that I was born a Catholic in a small town in Minnesota where the church was just one of several churches. Ecumenism was in the future, but we lived a kind of practical ecumenism of our own. We went to separate schools and churches but, Protestant and Catholic, we played together after school, and, as we grew older, dated and danced together. We went to the lawn socials at the Episcopal church, hoped for invitations to the Mason's annual Christmas dance, and invited our Protestant friends to midnight Mass. In summer we all went to Chautauqua meetings in a tent on the courthouse lawn, where we were regaled with a mixture of entertainment, temperance, and a sort of nondenominational American religion. Mixed marriages were deplored on both sides, and avoided in principle, but not uncommon. Most of us had both Catholic and Protestant relatives.

Thus, having been exposed all my life to the garden varieties of Episcopalians, Congregationalists (as they were then called), and Lutherans from an early age, I grew up knowing that we Catholics had no monopoly either on goodness or on certain kinds of moral blindness. We all failed the Christian vision in one way or another. And were not visibly more just or more kindly than were our few local agnostics.

It mattered, too, that our parish, once French, then French and Irish, then for the most part German—to be strictly accurate, what we called Luxemburger German, or Plattdeutsch—had such a mixture of Catholic heritages and the strengths of accommodation to the pioneer historical realities. The School Sisters of Notre Dame, who staffed our parochial grade school and high school, had, in my time, been teaching in coeducational high schools for three generations by the time the encyclical disapproving coeducation (if not condemning it) appeared. (One of the early nuns on the frontier had sensibly concluded that it was useless to teach girls if the boys were to grow up, as she put it, "barbarians."

After a costly struggle she had wrested from the authorities in the German mother house the permission to teach them both.) These sisters were good teachers and took pride in the fact that the school did so well in competitive state board examinations and in winning accreditation. The school, church, and convent rang with music—and good music, too.

It had, of course, not always been that way. There had been a slow progress from a small school designed primarily to safeguard the language and religion of German immigrants to a school with the goal of education for its own sake. The development was the result of conflict. The German pastors were less interested than the laity in adapting to American standards. My mother was sent to the public high school so that she could qualify for the university despite the thundering assertions of the autocratic monsignor that this action automatically excommunicated my grandmother. My grandmother was sure that it did no such thing and took horse and buggy to the next town, where the pastor supported her view.

I attach importance to the foregoing aspects of my personal history and to others like them because they had a part in shaping my attitude toward the Church. I had been born into my family and, inescapably, it was my family for good or ill. In the same way I had been born into the Church and it remained my Church for good or ill. Because there were so many underlying givens in the Catholicism of my little town, I was spared the illusions which so many contemporary and former Catholics seem to have shed so painfully. Our attitude toward the clergy, for example—personified for us in our parish priest, since we only saw a bishop once every few years —was that they were clearly human and fallible but necessary if we were to have a church at all.

Rosemary Haughton, the English writer on spirituality, has said that the mark of the present-day Catholic is the calm refusal to be read out of the Church if he or she disagrees in conscience with the magisterium. In former times disagreement on any one point would have been enough to cause a Catholic to think of himself or herself as "out of the Church." The current attitude was foreshadowed, it seems to me, long ago in the incidents I have detailed above: in the sisters adapting to coeducation, in my grandmother's well-mannered but calm defiance of the unreasonable monsignor. When the strictures of the Church were in conflict with common sense, we assumed that there was very probably more than one opinion to be cited. And, if not, one did what had to be done.

More important than any of this, however, was that in a little town one readily absorbs a realistic knowledge of good and evil in human nature and of human weakness. One learns to accept the fact that humankind is not easily transformed by grace. One sees the Church, without quite knowing it, as less a powerful institution than a struggling one. We rather liked the term "Mother Church," and, although we could not have phrased it that way, our reasons were probably the same as Karl Adam's:

And God permits so much weakness and wretchedness in the earthly Church because He is good. . . . For how might we, who are "prone to evil from our youth," who are constantly stumbling, constantly struggling, and never spotless . . . how might we adhere to a Church, which displayed holiness not as a chaste hope, but as a radiant achievement? . . . The Catholic does not desire some ideal Church. . . . Though his mother be travel-stained with long journeying, though her countenance be furrowed with care and trouble—yet, she is his mother. In her heart burns the ancient love. Out of her eyes shines the ancient faith. From her hands flow the ancient blessings. . . .

In contrast to the other religions practiced in our town, ours seemed rather more strenuous, active, and always interesting, forever facing us with challenges and tests of endurance. There were two Masses on Sunday, the High and the Low—one went to both if one wanted to receive communion, because the High Mass was never interrupted for that and we were all supposed to be at High Mass, which was offered for the parish. On almost every weekday there was a rather doleful requiem sung by us school children. It was in the day when Mass "offerings" were an important part of parish income. There were Rosary devotions twice a week in October and May, Stations of the Cross in Lent and, I think, in Advent too, liturgically strange as that may seem. There were processions to climax Forty Hours' Adoration and the Rogation Days, "visits" to be made on the Feast of Portiuncula and Holy Thursday. There was a satisfyingly exhausting Holy Week. There were missions, novenas, vespers, sodality meetings, choir practice—I marvel at the reminiscence.

All this pious activity ministered to, and nourished our appetite for the transcendent—was a reassurance to us, indeed, of the reality of the transcendent. It was a sign that above and beyond what we could see and know there was that which was grave, beautiful, unseen and unknowable, something woven through the threads of human history stretching back over the ages and to go on past the end of time. The practices have disappeared and I do not miss them, would see no need for them today, but the Church remains for me a sign of the transcendent. That is to say that the Church was my way to God, and I acknowledge the debt.

When novelist Herman Wouk set out to write *This Is My God*, he said that he was really writing about the Jewish way to him and that his book would irritate the person who was sure that God did not exist. My insistence on the transcendent will do the same thing. I am, therefore, grateful for his cogent defense of believers: "Now the belief in God may turn out at the last trump to be a mistake. Meantime, let us be quite clear, it is not merely the comfort of the simple though it is that, too, much to its glory—it is a formidable intellectual position with which most of the first class minds of the human race, century in and century out, have concurred, each in his own way."

When I was preparing to write this paper I came across another paper—evidently saved by a fond aunt—written when I was sixteen and entitled "What My Religion Means to Me." I wince now at the obvious pieties and the smug language, but I recognize the budding of some of the ideas which have grown and matured over the years.

I wrote, for example, of the family given me by the Church —the hosts of saints and martyrs. Actually I don't think I really knew very much about the saints then. The age of truthful biography and the editions of unexpurgated writings were still to come. But they were to me the counterpart of those who concurred in belief, as Wouk says, century after century, each in his own way. It has been a peculiarly Catholic pleasure to have that company at hand, accessible through prayer, giving depth and dimension to faith, refracting its light in a hundred nations and across time. There is in Chesterton's democracy of the dead that which gives a different lens view of history, dissents from the idolization of progress and the inevitable superiority of a technological vulture.

There was in that a preparation for what is only now beginning to be a popular apprehension—the sense, or the fear, that, as C. S. Lewis put it, "organic life is only a lightning flash in cosmic history. In the long run, nothing will come of it." This thought is so contrary to evolutionism (the word again I owe to Lewis), which has been our popular belief through much of the age we call modern, that it is very probably the basis of the current widespread alienation and despair. For evolutionism, says Lewis, evolution simply means improvement.

And it is not confined to organisms, but applied also to moral qualities, institutions, arts, intelligence and the like. There is thus lodged in popular thought the conception that improvement is, somehow, a cosmic law; a conception to which the sciences give no support at all. There is no general tendency for the universe as a whole to move in any direction which we shall call "good." There is no evidence that the mental and moral capacities of the human race have been increased since man became man. On the contrary, Evolution—even if, it were what the mass of people suppose it to be—is only (by astronomical and physical standards) an inconspicuous foreground detail in the picture. The huge background is filled by quite different principles: entropy, degradation, disorganization.

The saints, and all great human spirits less formally recognized, are, of course, glorious evidence that our mental and moral capacities have not increased. It would be as hard to improve on a first-century saint as on a twentieth-century one. Their persistent effort to grow in the love and knowledge of God and the love and service of our fellow humans because of, and in spite of, the fact that we have not here a lasting city heartens one to face the black holes of the universe.

It is only now that I realize that, as I was growing up, the *Weltanschauung* of the saints permeated the life around me. The people of my world did not really expect that life should be happy, but they did think it could be enjoyed. I was surrounded by those, especially among the members of my family and my teachers, whose lives were marked by self-sacrifice, faithfulness, long-suffering, patience, and hope in the face of overwhelming disappointment, cruel disease, and real want. Given the desperation of those Depression times, there was an astonishing amount of kindness shown and amazing efforts to make others happy. People said of others, "He is a good man," or, "Now she is really a good woman," and knew what they meant. Virtue was valued. In life as in the New Testament Jesus Christ, evidence of God, is seen in his effect on those who meet him.

I wrote also in that school paper of long ago what it meant to be, through the Church, part of twenty centuries of human history. And this was not a negligible factor in forming a world view. As Mary McCarthy was to write later, "If you are born and brought up a Catholic, you have absorbed a good deal of world history and the history of ideas before you are twelve, and it is like learning a language early; the effect is indelible." You are emotionally involved in that history because it is your own.

In later years the involvement with the saints was to lead me, through the mystics and a fascination with the science of prayer, to a sense of unity with many Asians. The involvement in the struggle of ideas became the basis for a deep interest in ecumenism. Because of the fortuitous way these interests matured and branched out in my own experience, I am convinced that one reason I remain a Catholic is a vivid sense that, in the words of St. Augustine, "the temple of God is still a-building"; "the house [of the Church] is now being constructed."

To me one of the most amazing growths in the Church and testimony that it is "still a-building" has been the growth of social consciousness. We live in an era in which priests, nuns, and lay persons are martyred by oppressive governments. They are imprisoned and tortured by totalitarian regimes now and in the past, not only because they hold to the faith as in former eras but *because they give voice to the poor.*

To judge by what I wrote, my sixteen-year-old self must have had a compartmentalized mind in this regard, and was apparently untroubled by it. I remember well that I, a Depression child and from a partisan and newspaper background, lived in an atmosphere of social change and upheaval. My high school Latin book of that same year is autographed by Floyd B. Olson, Minnesota's charismatic Farmer-Laborite governor; I had left school one day to hear him speak to a huddled group of impoverished farmers on a street corner. In my family we argued around the supper table about the rights of labor, the farm strikes, and forced bank holidays. We were beginning to be aware of discrimination against the Jews and of racial injustice. There is no evidence that we connected any of this with religion at that time.

I think we assumed good will on that part of the Church. She had followed poor immigrants to the cities and the farms of this country to console and be of service. A far-reaching step had been taken when Cardinal Gibbons, backed by most of the American bishops, secured Rome's reversal of the condemnation of the Knights of Labor in 1888. The Knights were the forerunners of the labor organizations at the center of social struggle in the thirties. The American Catholic workingman joining in the struggle for social justice with his peers of other traditions was, therefore, not condemned but assured that a Christian should be an advocate of that justice. The workers of this country had never been alienated wholly from the Christian churches as they had been in Europe.

Whether I knew this or not, throughout my college years my interest in social justice—and it was to become a passionate interest—did not seem to mesh with any interest in the Church. In fact it completely overrode it. Catholicism seemed to have little to do with the deep-lying problems of mass poverty and worldwide social and economic breakdown. The writers and speakers who addressed these problems with solutions leaned toward cooperative democracy, socialism, and Marxism. Young people were growing impatient. Some of my friends became communists; one of my classmates a Trotskyite. The only light on the scene seemed to be *The Catholic Worker*, newly founded by Peter Maurin and Dorothy Day. I thought it encouraging, but a bit odd. It was years before I could see that the *Worker* drew from the wellspring of the gospel a concept of justice more fundamental, more far-reaching, than the other movements I knew.

In a few years I was to take part in, and take hope from, the Catholic interracial movement, the liturgical movement, the rural life movement—so much of the trial and error and the ferment which was cut off by World War II and taken up, slightly altered, thereafter. There was the possibility, I began to perceive, of integrating spirituality and justice. But to no one movement do I owe as much as I do the *Worker*. As a young teacher I became a volunteer at the Catholic Worker House on Hennepin Island in Minneapolis, and wrote its newsletter, filling in for men who had been drafted. (Although the *Worker* preached pacifism, not all of the workers or the men who drifted to the houses were conscientious objectors.) I took in some of the attitudes of the *Worker*: that poverty was often not simply misfortune but a condition; that the poor had the right to privacy and dignity and should be subjected to neither questionnaires nor preaching; that the Church was ourselves and we had no need to wait for the lead of pope, bishops, or priests to follow the teachings of the gospel. If we acted, the Church was acting. So today when I am reminded that the bishops have never spoken out on racism and did not speak on Vietnam, I am impatient but relatively untroubled. Lay groups have, and did. In addition to the *Worker*, the National Catholic Conference for Interracial Justice and Catherine de Hueck's Friendship House movement worked against racism in the thirties, and the peace movements of that time foreshadowed the protests against the Vietnam war.

For the great majority, I suppose, all these concerns seem to have stemmed from Vatican II. The reverse is closer to the truth. Vatican II stemmed from these concerns and others like them. There had been signs on the horizon for a long time—in America a development in Catholic thought culminating in the American bishops' statement on social reconstruction in 1919, and in general an increasing tendency of social thinkers and moral theologians to converge in their application of moral principles to social trends.

The cataclysm of the Crash and the Great Depression called all complacency into question and there was a veritable explosion of action and concern. Spurred on by the social teaching in their colleges sparked by the thought developed at such places as the Institute for Social Order, young people moved into public life, not for the prestige and power to be found there in the "Hurrah" tradition of another era—for they had other professions open to them now—but out of social concern and a desire to serve. At this same time in the Catholic spectrum alone many new forms of service other than those I have mentioned were tried. The actual number of people affected might not have been great, but many were of leadership quality.

All this was made more meaningful for me, a young Catholic college teacher, because it was part of a sort of springtime in the Church. I had discovered as a teacher in the public schools and in my graduate-school experience that, if I did not think of the Church as an enemy of the intellect, there were many who did. Now the so-called Catholic Renaissance was at its joyful height. As I have written elsewhere of that time, "To be Catholic no longer meant that one kept one's religion in one mental compartment, one's secular knowledge in another. We had only begun to sense in my college days that the Depression in America and the fragmentation in Europe, accompanied by economic chaos there, had shattered faith in the inevitability of progress and the infallibility of science. Recurring wars, the rise of nazism and fascism, the questioning threat of communism, the growing awareness of economic and racial injustice in our own country—and now finally world war—all these had reawakened interest in the problem of evil.

"The Church was being rediscovered. To be a Catholic now meant that one was part of a worldwide community which shared a splendid heritage of arts and letters and in which tremendous intellectual effort was being put into the restructuring of human society to cope with modern evils. It meant that one could claim affinity with the ancient Greek and Roman and Hebraic cultures from which Christianity sprang; it meant that one could identify the universal in the tribal and ethnic cultures to which Christianity had adapted; it meant that one could affirm as Catholic everything true and good.

"The Church in America, at least in an important segment of its intellectual leadership, had rediscovered its pre-Puritan past and was no longer to be thought of as at odds with science and the arts. It was an era of conversions: Evelyn Waugh, Robert Lowell, Thomas Merton—and so many others. One could think of Christian thought as a dominant and creative influence once again in Western culture. Neo-Scholastic philosophers like Bergson, Gilson, and Maritain were seriously discussed in the most thoughtful journals.

"Waugh, Graham Greene, Bernanos, Mauriac, Claudel, were in vogue wherever the novel was seriously discussed—and they were ours. Gerard Manley Hopkins was one of the most imitated of poets, Sean O'Faolain, Sean O'Casey, Paul Vincent Carroll, and Frank O'Connor might be deplored in their native Ireland, but they were applauded and discussed here.

James Joyce was perceived as permanently formed by the Catholicism he rejected, as were others whose battle with guilt was a testimony of an inverse sort. A minor school of the breed known to us as 'Catholic authors,' as distinguished from authors who merely happened to be Catholic, flourished briefly; among them we counted Paul Horgan, Richard Sullivan, Riley Hughes, Harry Sylvester, Joseph Dever—and perhaps the most distinguished, J. F. Powers, whose short stories brought the near perfection of that most American of forms to the service of what we thought of as truly Catholic themes. . . ."

It was, in part, a false springtime. It was too full of certainties, even triumphal. Yet it was so widespread and so much an evidence of the diffusion of higher education within a century that it gave promise of the coming into being for the first time since the Reformation of what Erasmus hoped for when he spoke of the *respublica literatorum.* That the names of the writers above—especially the philosophers—are all lay names is testimony to the way in which the teaching Church was becoming the whole Church.

There was also in that springtime a foretaste of what a truly Christian humanism might be like, that humanism which Hans Küng defines as seen in the light of "this Jesus," "the concrete criterion," "the Christ." "In his light they think they cannot support just any kind of humanism which simply affirms all that is good, beautiful, true, and human. But they can support a truly radical humanism which is able to integrate and cope with what is not true, not good, unlovely, inhuman; not only everything positive—and here we discern what a humanism has to offer—everything negative, even suffering, sin, death, futility."

I glimpsed that humanism once and the Church was at its center, but it was *in action* and in much of its theory the humanism of the lay Christian. Even the social movements which have had lasting effect and which continue today were lay in inspiration and execution. Clerics in these movements were for the most part ministers, perhaps guides, but serving the faithful. This was an amazing growth in the concept of

Church and it had taken place in less than a century. Many of the more avant-garde groups forming today have no distinctions at all between clergy and laity and religious—that may indicate further growth. Other groups stressing lay spirituality select from the group clergy as needed.

When, as I began to write, I asked the most activist of my three daughters why she thought I remained a Catholic and an involved one, she fixed me with an astonished stare. "Obviously because nothing else in the world has such potential." If one of the young who refuses to have anything to do with the visible Church feels that strongly about its promise for the world, I must accept that the promise is there and tangible still. It may be possible that the Church will yet be as Cardinal Suhard, archbishop of Paris, once hoped: "It will perhaps be the great honor of our time to have started what others carry through; a humanism in proportion to the world in God's plan. On this condition and only this condition can the Church develop and become in the near future what she was in the Middle Ages for the West, the spiritual center for the world."

If, of late, the Church, at least the juridical Church, seems turned in on itself, obsessed with its own divisions, with its hierarchy, clergy, and orders, with defections, its prophetic voice uncertain, weakened rather than strengthened by change—well, that is an unhappy, unexpected negative effect of the Council, but not necessarily a lasting one.

It is increasingly clear to me as I write and reflect on my experience that the idea of *church* changed for me long ago. Social action for me had led inevitably to ecumenism. Young Catholics of my time who moved out into the arena of politics in the spirit of the renewal or who encountered the world in one or more of the various social movements made common cause with their Protestant and Jewish brethren moved by the same concerns. There was no longer one right way; there was only *the way*. For Christians this meant that the invisible Church was already one. They thus anticipated the *Decree on Ecumenism* of Vatican II, as is readily acknowledged in the words of that decree: "Cooperation among all

Christians vividly expresses that bond which already unites them, and it sets in clearer relief the feature of Christ the servant. Such cooperation . . . already exists in many countries . . ."

Church has come to mean for me the community of *all* believers who follow Christ in this world. It can also be used to designate believers with a common system of government. Theologians hold that these are mysteriously one. We used to speak of the Church Triumphant—that is, the Church in heaven—and the Church Militant, the Church on earth. But, as Abbot Butler points out in the Foreword to his book *The Idea of the Church*, the name "church" was originally given to the community here and now, the community of believers in the world. The church we know as "Catholic" may be the core of the Church in the world; it may be at one side acting as counterpoise; but it is, I feel, essential in making visible that great community.

In the end to choose the Church is an act of faith. I wrote rather emotionally but with some genuine feeling in that high school paper, "If I were to be deprived of my religion I would be deprived of life. What it would mean—no Communion, no Mass!" I am a Catholic because, above all, it is the Church of the Eucharist. Butler says, "I have been ready, especially in the later pages of this book, to fall back on the more thoroughly Christian term [for church] 'communion' which has the great merit of presenting the Church in her true colours as a fraternity of charity, and suggesting that the real heart of her unity is in the sacrament of Holy Communion."

The Eucharist is the link with Jesus the founder and head. The disciples knew him in the breaking of the bread. With the Eucharist, I once read, he flung himself into the current of our affairs until the end of time. He gives us to eat. Manna. Living Bread. Bread of the strong. Sustenance of the weak. Living presence. In bad times the Eucharist is the sign of the community which should exist, in good times the celebration of the Church living, growing, becoming.

WHY I AM A CATHOLIC

Fulton J. Sheen

The most widely recognized and beloved Catholic prelate of twentieth-century America, Archbishop Fulton J. Sheen has had distinguished careers as radio and television commentator, as lecturer, as author, and above all as priest. His radio and television programs were carried by hundreds of stations with a weekly audience in the tens of millions. His lectures are as popular as ever, and his sermons and retreats always attract overflow crowds. He has written some sixty books, which have sold millions of copies, among them *Life of Christ, Life Is Worth Living, Peace of Soul, Lift Up Your Heart, Those Mysterious Priests,* and *The World's First Love.* Recipient of numerous honorary degrees and awards, he was national director of the Society for the Propagation of the Faith for sixteen years, bishop of Rochester in 1966–69 and is now titular archbishop of Newport, Wales. Now in his eighties, he is as active as ever, preaching and delivering retreats all over the world.

I must state immediately that I am not a Catholic for the same reason that I am a biped. I was born with two legs. I was not born an adopted son of God. No one is *born* a Catholic. One *becomes* or is begotten a Catholic by a gift of God. We *make* things that are unlike us: A carpenter makes a table. But we *beget* that which is like us: Parents beget a child. To be *made* by God as a Creator is not the same as being begotten by God through His Grace.

St. Paul said his becoming a member of the Church was like having an "abnormal birth"; "I had persecuted the church of God. . . . However, by God's grace I am what I am" (1 Cor. 15:8, 9–10). When I was a small boy, my parents gave me some leaden soldiers for Christmas. I lined them up on a red carpet in the living room and wondered what it would be like if each one of those leaden soldiers became a real live soldier. I could almost sense the smell of musketry; the red of the carpet became the red of the battlefield. There was nothing in the leaden soldiers which could possibly elevate them to the human level, nor by their own power or capacity could they become other than they were. Some energy outside of their leadenness would have been required to raise their dignity to that of human nature.

So I am not a Catholic in virtue of my intelligence or my own good works, whether they be great or small. I am a Catholic because the Lord, through no merits of mine, willed to lift me from the weak and fallen human state to that of sharing His Divine Life. Nor does the Lord always choose the best: "Think what sort of people you are, whom God has called. Few of you are men of wisdom, by any human standard; few are powerful or highly born. Yet, to shame the wise, God has chosen what the world counts folly, and to shame what is strong, God has chosen what the world counts weakness. He has chosen things low and contemptible, mere nothings, to overthrow the existing order. And so there is no place for human pride in the presence of God" (1 Cor. 1:26–29).

This point is illustrated by the story of Nicodemus, who appears only at night in the Gospel, maybe because he was afraid of being seen with Our Lord, or because he wished to be unseen by his strict brethren of the Pharisees. A great personage he was: one of the leaders of the Jews and a member of the Jewish Council that governed the strictly internal affairs of the nation. Christ Himself called him a "teacher of Israel," which suggests considerable expertise in religious matters. When Nicodemus came to Our Lord, he said he was impressed by the signs and wonders which He did. The answer of the Lord was that the signs and miracles were not really important but what was important was a change in man's inner life which could only be described as a new birth.

When Nicodemus was told that he must be *born again*, it meant that there would have to be a radical change in him which could only be described as being born all over again. But to Nicodemus this was impossible, for he was thinking of being born again in terms of biology. "How is it possible," asked Nicodemus, "for a man to be born when he is old? Can he enter into his mother's womb a second time and be born?" Jesus answered, "In truth, I tell you, no one can enter the kingdom of God without being born from water and spirit. Flesh can give birth only to flesh; it is spirit that gives birth to spirit" (John 3:4–5). Water is the symbol of cleansing; the implication is that when God takes possession of our lives and when we love Him with all our heart, sins of the past are forgiven and forgotten. The Spirit is the symbol of power. There enters into us a new dynamism, which enables us to do what by our own fleshly powers we could never do. This gift by which we are given a new birth, a new creation and a rule by the Spirit instead of the flesh, is what is called *Grace*—because it is *gratis* and because it does not proceed from man himself but from above. The deep profound and ultimate answer to the question, Why am I a Catholic? is: I am a Catholic through the Grace and the Goodness of God.

Once it is recognized that one is a Catholic by the Grace of God, it still remains possible for reason and experience to justify the choice. It is one thing to receive an inheritance to which we were not entitled, and another thing to keep it invested wisely; it is one thing to receive a talent, like the gift of music to Mozart, who heard melodies all at once, and another thing to practice, train, and develop that talent; it is one thing to receive a gold mine, and it is quite another matter to refine the gold so that it may become more valuable and more beautiful; it is one thing to be born with a good physique as an athlete, it is another matter to train and discipline oneself to ensure victory on the field.

Each one who has received the gift has many different points of view to support it. As St. Peter wrote, "Be always ready with your defense whenever you are called to account for the hope that is in you, but make that defense with modesty and respect" (1 Pet. 3:15).

The three principal reasons that I would give for being a Catholic are because the Catholic Church is the lover of: (1) life; (2) truth; (3) love.

1. The Church Is the Lover of Life

I am a Catholic because I believe there ought to be a higher life than the human. Regardless of all the biological refinements of the body, it is not logical to assume that evolution should stop with man. The chemical order which embraces iron, hydrogen, oxygen, phosphorus, etc. has no activity within itself. A diamond ring will not move except by some power outside itself. We have the first beginnings of life wherever there is some activity from *within*. The plant does not grow by the addition of part to part, as a house grows by the addition of brick to brick, but by the expansion of some vital elements within so that the plant is able to generate other plants and grow and nourish itself. Animal life is higher than plant life because it has an added double interior activity—namely locomotion, and the power of sense perception. Mounting a step higher in the hierarchy of creation, we find that man has a new kind of inner movement or immanence above plants and animals—namely, the activity of thinking and willing. He can conceive or generate thoughts such as "justice" or "peace"; these do not drop from his mind as fruit from a tree. A stone has no will. It is in servile obedience to the law of gravitation. But man has the power of choice and the ability to elect ends and purposes. A bird never improves the building of its nest nor changes its style from the Roman to the piercing piety of Gothic, but human nature can set up a target and direct the arrows of the will toward it. Every time we say "thank you," we are refuting determinism and implying that something could be done which might have been left undone.

Why should this upward thrust of evolution with its increasing interior activity cease with the human being? If chemicals can enter into the life of plants, if plants can enter into the life of animals, and if chemicals, plants, and animals can be taken into the life of man for his perfection, *why should there not be some higher life to which human nature could be assimilated?* We have no more right to say there is no higher life above us than a rose has a right to say there is no life above it.

But there is a catch here in the sense that chemicals cannot ordinarily and over a short span acquire the life of plants, nor can plants become animals, nor can an animal be made a man. In the ordinary processes of nature, before a lower kingdom can be taken into a higher kingdom, the latter must *come down* to it and elevate it to its new realm. Animals must go down to plant life, and man must go down to all the lower kingdoms before they can ever enter his kingdom of thinking and loving. So too, if there is any sense to evolution, there must also be a point where a life higher than the human comes down to him to lift him up, to give new powers, and infuse into him a more intense immanent activity. This breakthrough of Divinity into humanity took place when God became man in the person of Christ. He thus explained the purpose of His coming: "I have come that men may have life, and may have it in all its fullness" (John 10:10). Over and above human life in all of its richness is the Divine Life of God Himself which Christ brought to us in the incredible littleness of His breakthrough in Bethlehem.

The next big question is how that Divine Life is made available to us. It is not forced upon us, for neither love nor gifts are ever forced. It is made available in somewhat the same way as Christ became present in His Mother. Through an angel she was asked if she would give God a human nature. For centuries He had been expected, but her immediate problem was that she was a virgin. Being assured that the Holy Spirit would provide the generation rather than a man, she agreed to give God a manhood. *So every person in the world is given an opportunity to answer the same question that Mary was asked:* "Will you give Christ your human nature?" As He took a human nature from her and used it as the instrument of His Divinity, so He wishes to take our human nature in order to "divinize" us. The change that He makes in us would be something like a leaden soldier becoming a man or a rag doll becoming a little girl. There is nothing in our poor humanity which could ever divinize us unless Divinity came down from above and transformed and transmuted us by a gift of Divine Life. That is why this higher life is called "Grace"; it is a free gift of God.

Once we are given our human nature, Christ uses it as we use a pencil as the instrument of our human spirit. If I wish to write the word "God," it will do so because it is obedient to my personal will. If the pencil, however, had a will of its own and I wanted to write the word "God" and it wrote the word "dog," I could do nothing with it. So the surrender of our intellect and will to Christ becomes the condition of His using us as the instrument of His Divinity. Once we make the surrender, we become "other Christs."

But God did not become man merely to sanctify individuals. If a thousand persons share in His Divine Life, then they already form a community or a corporate life. Their prayer then becomes not "My Father" but "Our Father," for as Christ is the natural Son of God, so we are the adopted sons of God. All partakers of His Divine nature are like cells in this body. As my body is made up of millions and millions of cells and they are all one because vivified by one soul, governed by one visible head, and presided over by one invisible mind, so, too, all who are "in Christ" form one body or Church or people of God because they are vivified by one soul, which is the Holy Spirit, and become governed by the invisible mind of Christ in heaven and are presided over by a visible head on earth, who is the successor of Peter.

This corporate life is not an institution, it is a mystery. As Christ had a Divine and a human nature, so His extended body or the Church has a visible and an invisible side. The visible side and sometimes the all too human aspect of it is its poor members; the invisible aspect is the Christ life, which is preserved principally in two ways—by Word and by Sacraments. The Word is the reception of the truth that He preached. The Sacraments are seven signs by which He pours Divine life into our elevated human nature at various stages from birth to death.

Certainly the Church has many imperfections and even scandals. But there was a "scandal" in the earthly life of Our Blessed Lord: How could He who is God ever suffer such a defeat as Calvary? How could the Omnipotent be bound with cord and fastened to a Cross? This scandal He overcame by the Resurrection. As there were *physical* scandals in the life of Christ, so there are spiritual, moral and mystical scandals in the Church. But they do not touch its substance, which is Divine. As the Lord on the Cross did not have a single bone broken though His flesh was torn in shreds, so the Church in its essence is holy though some of its cells may be unholy. From one point of view a hospital is an evil place: In it one hears shrieks of pain and sees agony, blood, pus, and disease. But from another point of view there is curing, healing, caring, and loving.

The further evidence of the love of the Church for life is to be found in the three meanings that are attached to the "body" in Sacred Scripture. The body, first of all, refers to the physical Body of Christ, which was the instrument of His Divinity; through it He taught, He governed, and He sanctified. The "body" also may mean an ecclesial unity of all who are one in Christ, which is the Church. This identity is so close that, after Christ ascended into heaven, Paul, who began persecuting the Church, heard the risen Christ say to him, "Why are you persecuting me?" If someone steps on your foot, your head complains. Paul was touching the body of Christ and the head complained, thus showing that the Church is His Body and the risen Christ is the Head and they are one. Thirdly, the word "body" may stand for the Eucharistic Body, and here it may either be a sacrifice or a sacrament. In the Mass the sacrifice of Christ is prolonged through our human nature. He can die only once, but He has imposed on us the law that unless there is a Good Friday in our lives there will never be an Easter Sunday. The Mass is the lifting of the Cross from Calvary and planting it in New York, Saigon, Paris, and Nairobi in order that we might unite our sacrificial living with His death, saying in union with Him, "This is my Body, this is my Blood." The Eucharist is, therefore, a union not only with the life of Christ but also with His death.

But in addition to being a sacrifice, the Eucharist is also a sacrament by which His presence is prolonged on the altar, thus giving the Church a sense of holiness which otherwise would be missing to a mere building. One of the reasons that so many are found visiting in a Catholic church at any hour of the day and sometimes at night is that all Catholics believe that Christ is really and truly present in the tabernacle, as His presence was foretold in the Old Testament in the "Bread of Presence" on the altar of Israel.

The Church's love of life extends to the very beginning of human life; hence she is opposed to abortion, to destruction of human life in the womb. She upholds the sanctity of life in all of its forms and holds that the unity of love and creative aspects of marriage cannot be separated. It is true that nature does separate sex as a manifestation of marital love and generation, for not every union of husband and wife produces new life. It would be quite wrong, however, to say that because nature separates, it would, therefore, be right for a married couple to deliberately prevent the act of generation. In marriage "what God unites, let no man put asunder." Nature may do things which man may not do. Nature puts an end to every human life, but not even a Hitler may legitimately do that. Nature sometimes spreads diseases, floods cities, and spontaneously sets fires, but man may not do these things.

When Paul VI published his letter *Humanae Vitae*, it was, first of all, an affirmation of a continuity of love and life, of planting and reaping the harvest. As those who eat at table may not do so just for the pleasure of eating more and disgorge their food into a vomitorium as did the Romans, so there may not be deliberate frustration of life just for the sake of carnal pleasure. It was interesting to observe the negative reaction to the Church's defense of human life and the response it provoked in a civilization whose best sellers are "The Joys of Sex" or "What You Did Not Know About Sex Until Now." In the world many otherwise good men and women will defend the taking of life and consider suitable for a marriage bed those things which an older generation knew to be found only in a brothel. One wonders with Malcolm Muggeridge (in *Christ and the Media*, p. 58) if modern man is not out to destroy himself:

Surveying and weighing up the whole scene, then, will not the final conclusion be that western man decided to abolish himself, creating his own boredom out of his own affluence, his own vulnerability out of his own strength, his own impotence out of his neurotomania, himself blowing the trumpet that brought the walls of his own city tumbling down, and having convinced himself that he was too numerous, laboring with pill, and scalpel and syringe to make himself fewer, until at last, having educated himself into imbecility, polluted and drugged himself into stupefaction, he keeled over, a weary, battered old Brontosaurus and became extinct.

In summary, T. S. Eliot, in "The Choruses from the Rock," asks:

Why should men love the Church? Why should they love her laws?
She tells them of Life and Death, and of all that they would forget.
She is tender where they would be hard, and hard where they like to be soft.
She tells them of Evil and Sin, and other unpleasant facts.
They constantly try to escape
From the darkness outside and within
By dreaming of systems so perfect that no one will need to be good.

2. The Church Is the Lover of Truth

Truth does not seem to be held in much higher esteem now than it was in the days when Pilate brought Our Blessed Lord before the howling mob. The Prisoner before him had said, "I am the Truth" (John 14:6). No one before in history ever made that claim. All religious and social leaders had rather suggested following a code or a rule or a set of precepts in order to know the truth. Our Blessed Lord identified Himself and Truth. Truth becomes lovable only when it is discovered in a person. No one can fall in love with an abstraction or a syllogism or a code. That is one of the basic reasons also why good example is such a strong affirmation of truth; when that fails, others have a right to say, "I cannot hear what you say because I see the way you live." When Pilate heard Our Blessed Lord say, "My task is to bear witness to the truth. For this was I born" (John 18:37), he replied, "What is truth?" and turned his back on it with a sneer, as if he had studied pragmatism under William James.

Truth is related to objectivity and implies a correspondence between the mind and reality. Today truth and goodness are reduced to sentiments and attitudes which are presumed to be reflections of the way society lives. One justification for doing what is wrong is "Everybody's doing it." If 53 per cent of motorists drove through red lights and 56 per cent of the people took heroin, both would be presumed to be right. The false assumption behind this is that man creates values and, hence society can choose an ideology or a code very much in the way that clothes are chosen. Truth is sometimes reduced to: "I *feel* it to be true." Never before was truth so much put at the mercy of an upset stomach or the need of Rolaids as it is when one subjective point of view decides that a foot shall measure fourteen inches instead of twelve.

Once the test of truth is put in subjective values, two consequences follow—one in democracy and the other in Communism. Democracy is inclined to believe that the majority makes things right, forgetful that it was a majority that sent Christ to the Cross and that the Holy Spirit on Pentecost appeared only to a minority. Democracy assumes that change or progress does away with absolute standards, forgetful of the fact that one can never know whether one is making progress unless there is a fixed point to measure against. Even in the scientific realm the theory of relativity is grounded upon the fact of time as the absolute measurement. Under Communism one must pretend to believe in patent falsehoods; as Boris Pasternak put it: "The great majority of us are required to live a life of systematic duplicity. Your health is bound to be affected if, day by day, you say the opposite of what you feel, if you grovel before what you dislike and rejoice at what brings you nothing but misfortune."

Truth does not depend on moods or on Gallup polls or on chronological snobbery such as "Times have changed." Right is right even if nobody is right, wrong is wrong even if everybody is wrong.

I am a Catholic because I believe in Truth and the Truth is in the Church. When Christ, the Son of God, came to this earth, He considered all three possible forms of Church government and finally decided on one. Entering the territory of

Caesarea Philippi, He first asked His disciples concerning the democratic form of Church government. He inquired from them the results of the Gallup poll concerning His identity: "Who do *men* say that the Son of Man is?" (Matt. 16:13). They could have answered in terms of a survey: To paraphrase the Gospel, 13 per cent say that you are John the Baptist, 22 per cent that you are Elijah, and 41 per cent that you are Jeremiah; the other 24 per cent say that you are one of the prophets. Leave the question of the Divinity of Christ to democratic processes and you get only contrary and contradictory answers for which the Lord had nothing but the withering scorn of His silence.

Next He appealed to the aristocratic form of Church government, to His House of Lords, to His Senate, to His Congress, to His apostles: "And you, who do you say I am?" (16:15). There was no answer, first of all, because no one had been made a spokesman: Furthermore, Judas had wandering thoughts about his financial sagacity; James and John were wondering if they might eventually be placed in positions of honor; Andrew had little concern about the problem, for he was the public relations official of the apostolic group, always introducing strangers to the Lord, such as his brother Peter and the boy with the fishes; then there was the Zealot, who wondered when Christ was going to drive the Romans out of Jerusalem. The Lord did not accept the aristocratic or the synodal or the congressional concept of the Church.

There is one other form of Church government left—namely, the theocratic, in which one man would be Divinely chosen and be guaranteed freedom from error. The one He chose was not necessarily the strongest of all. But he who was chosen, Simon Peter, stepped out from the apostolic group and, without their consent or consultation with them, gave the right answer to the question of the Lord: "You are the Messiah, the Son of the Living God."

How did he know? Jesus said to him, "Simon son of Jonah, you are favored indeed! You did not learn that from mortal man; it was revealed to you by my heavenly Father. And I say this to you: You are Peter, the Rock; and on this

Rock I will build my church, and the powers of death shall never conquer it. I will give you the keys of the kingdom of heaven: What you forbid on earth shall be forbidden in heaven, and what you allow on earth shall be allowed in heaven" (Matt. 16:17–20).

Peter was not naturally a rock; from the point of view of earthly heritage he was more like quicksand. He was constantly making promises to the Lord which he could never keep; he boasted of his natural powers which failed in a crisis. He was something like a weakling boy I knew when I was in the fifth grade who never took part in any athletics—a good wind would have blown him over; we called him "Hercules." I think Our Blessed Lord called Peter the Rock in sharp contrast to what he was by nature. But he would become a rock through Divine assistance and Divine illumination. That was the point.

Immediately after Christ told him that he would be preserved from error, Peter fell into sin and was called personally by Our Blessed Lord "Satan." That is because he tempted Our Lord from the Cross, which is the essence of the satanic. In this one scene distinction was made between infallibility and impeccability. Acting under divine guidance, Peter and Christ's Church would be preserved from error or the gates of hell. But, left to himself and his own resources, he could be a devil.

Later on, at the close of His life, the Lord speaking to the twelve singled out Peter: "Simon, Simon, take heed: Satan has been given leave to sift all of you like wheat; but for you I have prayed that your faith may not fail; and when you have come to yourself, you must lend strength to your brothers" (Luke 22:31–32). Our Blessed Lord here implies that the twelve whom He had just said "stood firmly by me in my times of trial" would be sorely tempted by the demonic; then the Lord prays not for the twelve but only for Peter: "I have prayed for thee that thy faith may not fail." As a result of that prayer of Christ to preserve Peter, he in turn is to strengthen the rest of the apostolic band. It is only the apostles and their successors throughout history who share in the prayer of Christ against the forces of evil and only when they are associated with Peter and his successors— never when they are separated from Him, even though they be an apostolic group.

Another evidence of the uniqueness of the position of Peter is that there was only one time in the life of Our Blessed Lord when He ever used the term "we" in relationship to a creature. Even when He taught the "Our Father," He never told us to call God "my Father." He was the natural son of God; we are the adopted children. When *you* pray, you say *Our* Father. But He told Peter that by fishing he would find the silver coin with which to pay the taxes, adding, "It will meet the tax for us both" (Matt. 17:26–27). This uniqueness of Peter in relationship to Christ is confirmed by the fact that he is the one who will, visibly and excluding all others, be the shepherd of the sheep (John 21:15–17), the one who possesses the power of Keys of the Kingdom. In this scene at the seashore after the Resurrection Our Blessed Lord uses two different words in the commission to Peter. One word in the original Greek, *boskein*, means to give food or to feed; the other word, *poimainein*, means to shepherd, to lead, to rule or to direct as a ruler. Peter had the direct duty of feeding the lambs, the lay folk or laity; but toward the sheep—that is to say, the bishops and priests—he had the duty of leading. The Savior's function as visible Shepherd over His visible flock on earth, which was now drawing to an end, was transferred by Him to St. Peter.

Thus the Head Shepherd, before withdrawing His visible presence, appointed another visible shepherd of the whole flock. Our Lord never intended that this double duty should die with Peter, for the Lord said that He would be with His Church "until the end of time." If the Church was to continue, then certainly the method of government which Christ associated with the Church was also to continue. The guarantees of truth which Christ gave to the Church did not die with Peter, but after his crucifixion rose again in Linus, Cletus, Clement of Rome and is still extant in that See which was set up by Peter. The Rock chosen by Christ, or the Key-Bearer, is still opening and closing the door; the

Leader is still strengthening his brethren; the Shepherd is still feeding and leading and dying for his lambs.

The love of the Church for the Truth does not mean that the Church has the right to proclaim new truths independent of Scripture and tradition. Infallibility is not a positive gift; it is negative: The Lord promised to preserve the Church from error. The teaching office of the Church is not a faucet that one turns on to learn truths of geography and science and literature; it is rather like the banks of the river or the levee which prevents the river from overflowing and ruining the countryside. The teaching office of the Vicar of Christ and the Hierarchy receives no Divine inspiration whatever to propose to the Church new truths. Furthermore, the bishops, whether individually or assembled in a council, and the Pope himself are obliged like everyone else to seek them out in Scripture as interpreted by the general sense of tradition. And though the responsibility of proclaiming the truth authoritatively belongs to the Church in its Vicar and in the bishops, the function of witnessing to this truth may fall to the Christians who are inspired by the Holy Spirit. St. Thomas Aquinas, the most learned of theologians, and St. Jerome, the biblical scholar, were not bishops. One of the most striking witnesses to the truth in critical times was St. Thomas More on the occasion of the schism of Henry VIII.

The most general misunderstanding of the authority of the Church is to set it off against the Bible as a rule of faith. As a matter of fact, there are two living or oral transmissions which are irreducible—the one coming from Christ and the apostles to the primitive Church, and the other coming from the primitive Church to us. Thus, the deposit revealed by Christ and the apostles to the primitive Church comes to us both by oral or written transmission—that is to say, by tradition and Scripture. Both of these, tradition and Scripture, descend to us by another living channel of transmission which implies divine assistance and the guidance of the Holy Spirit and that is the *magisterium* of the Church.

The truth of the Church is communicated through Scripture, tradition, and the magisterium as a threefold channel by

which the Word of God reaches us. Tradition is important
because the Church has a past; to ignore the wisdom of other
centuries would be to suffer from amnesia and to become a
victim of the idolatry of the contemporary. Nor will tradition
alone be the guide; otherwise there would be a petrifaction
and a slavery to the past. The Church declares the Divine
Revelation through the interior direction of the Holy Spirit,
who was given to her as her teacher. Thus the Catholic looks
to the magisterium or teaching office of the Church not in
order to avoid contact in depth with the Church's tradition
nor to excuse him from a study of Scripture but to enjoy the
mutual support and the confirming and elucidating and exalt-
ing power of the combination of all three. Scripture is indeed
the Word of God, but it can be interpreted in a thousand
different ways, as the multiplicity of sects within Christianity proves. Without tradition and the magisterium of the
Church we would not be able to determine the real meaning
which Scripture ought to have.

The Church, then, is not just an institution; it is a mystery, made up of visible and invisible elements as the Word
Incarnate was both Divine and human in unity of His Person.
To say, "I do not want a church or a pontiff or a bishop
standing between Christ and me," is like saying that I do not
want a Supreme Court and a Congress and a President to
stand between the authority of the United States and me.
These three bodies are the government of the United States
and derive their power from the consent of the governed.
The Church is even less of an intermediary, because her authority comes not from below, as in human government, but
from God. The Church does not come between Christ and
me. The Church is Christ, *the total permanent Christ of the
centuries*. The human instruments of Christ are, therefore, to
be judged not by themselves but by Him Who sent them in
His Name, just as the general is not to be judged by the tone
of his voice but by his right to command: "He that heareth
you, heareth Me," said Our Lord.

It may happen that the human failings of one exercising
authority may make it difficult to envisage Christ speaking

through him, but that should not make us doubt that Christ speaks, any more than the static on our radio makes us doubt the tones of the one who speaks from the studio are clear and distinct. If we are shocked at hearing that the Church must be intolerant about truth committed to her, it is because we have lost all respect for the uniqueness of truth. It is too generally assumed that tolerance is always right and intolerance always wrong. This is not really so. Tolerance and intolerance apply to two different things. Tolerance applies to persons, but never to principles; intolerance applies to principles, but not to persons. Because the butcher adds forty and forty to make one hundred and twenty, we become very intolerant about his mathematics, but we do not cut off his head. Nothing is as fearfully exclusive as truth, for truth is of God's making and not ours.

On the other hand, we have to be tolerant of persons, for they are human and liable to err. Most bigots are not to blame; they hate only because they've never been given an opportunity to know. I am sure that if I were trained on as much false history as some of them, had learned the same lies about the Church since childhood, and never had been given an opportunity to know the Church firsthand, I would probably hate it a thousand times more than they do. They do not really hate the Church; they only hate what they mistakenly believe to be the Church. The Church is only the trustee of the talents which Christ has bequeathed to it, and when the Bridegroom comes we must return to Him the original deposit of truth and also show interest on it in the increased harvest of the souls that have been saved.

This triple safeguard of truth in the Scriptures, tradition, and the teaching authority of the Church instead of enslaving actually makes the members of the Church free. As Our Blessed Lord said, "The truth will make you free." Aviators are free to fly only on condition that they respect the law of gravity. We are free to use words only on condition that we accept the standard meaning of those words in the dictionary. We are free to drive automobiles on condition that we obey the traffic laws. Every traveler who follows a road submits to the restriction of his freedom. But in submitting to the limitation of the road, he finds he is more free to travel it. The Church, in like manner, does not dam up the river of thought. She does not build great walls around rocky islands in the sea to prevent our children from playing; she builds them to prevent our children from falling into the sea and thus making all play impossible.

The more I submit myself to the truths of geography, the more free I am to travel; the more I reject the truths of history, the more I become enslaved to ignorance. When I obey the truths of the teaching authority of the Church, I no more relinquish my freedom than I do when I submit my speech to the laws of grammar. If it be said that the Catholic is enslaved to the Church, it is true in one sense, that he is enslaved to the Kingship of Christ. But that one point is like the fixed point of a pendulum, and from it we swing in beautiful rhythm with the freedom of Him who can make us free from everything, except the glorious liberty of the children of God or the freedom to become a saint.

How this works out practically can be seen in the response members of the Church have made to Communism, which would demand absolute obedience to an ideology. Loyalty to the Church is challenged as a disloyalty to civil authority. Consider the example of the Chinese priest Tong Che-tche, who was condemned by the Chinese authorities at Chungking on June 2, 1951. Before dying, he said to the Communists, "Today, a movement which has drawn up outside the Catholic Hierarchy is urging us to attack him who represents the Pope, who represents Jesus Christ. Gentlemen, I have only one soul and I cannot divide it up; but I have a body which can be divided up. It seems to me that the best thing to do is to offer my whole soul to God and the Holy Church, and my body to my country. . . . since I cannot remedy [the conflict in which Church and State are opposed], there is nothing I can do better than to offer my soul to one side and my body to the other, in sacrifice in the hope of promoting understanding between them. . . . I am a Chinese Catholic. I love my country; I love also my Church. I dissociate myself from everything that is opposed to the laws of my country just as I dissociate myself from everything that is opposed to the laws of my Church, and above all things I dissociate myself from everything which can sow discord. But if the Church and the government cannot come to an agreement, sooner or later every Chinese Catholic will have nothing left to do but die. Then why should one not offer one's body at once to hasten the mutual understanding of the parties concerned."

3. The Church Is the Lover of Love

The English language has only one word for love. This means confusion worse confounded because of the different meanings attached to love—e.g., "I love pickles," "I love soccer," "I love the New York Yankees," "I love art," "I love God." There really ought to be a profound difference between these various kinds of love. And there is. The Greeks had three different words for love—*eros*, *philia*, and *agape*. *Eros* meant "being in love" or friendship. Freud, however, changed the *eros* into the erotic, so that in popular language love became identified with sex. The fig leaf which was once placed over the private parts of our first parents to hide their shame is now put over the face; the person who is loved does not matter; it is the experience which counts. Drink the water, forget the glass. The ego is projected into the ego of another, creating the impression that the person is loved, when all that is really loved is the pleasure which the other person gives. This has been well expressed by a phrase in Orwell's 1984, "do you enjoy it." There is no reference to a person.

Sex is replaceable. Love is not. Sex may have been a taboo in Victorian days, but now it has been supplanted by the new taboo of death. When the purpose of life is lost, then love becomes identified with the erotic; the intensity of the experience is used to atone for the absence of a purpose or a fixed goal in life, just as people drive faster when they are lost in their automobiles. Because modern love is directed primarily to the sensation, many a man will say, "I want a woman," when what he wants is some apparatus to release his tension.

Philia is not just so much the love of an individual for an individual but of a person for a family, a nation, a tribe, a race, or humanity. The name Philadelphia is taken from two Greek words—*adelphos*, which means brother, and *philia*, which means love. As a noun *philia* is used only once in the New Testament. Like *eros* it lacks universality. Plato used it in his *Republic* to explain love of fellow citizens, but he did not include slaves.

The third Greek word for love, which has no English equivalent, is *agape*. It had no fixed meaning in classical Greek, but the New Testament writers needed a new word which was different from *eros* and *philia* to explain God's love for man especially the love of the Father, who gave His Son in order to save humanity. The famous chapter thirteen of First Corinthians makes *agape* greater than prophecies and mystery, and St. Paul wrote this letter in the city of Aphrodite, goddess of love, to indicate its transcendence above all earthly loves. *Agape* love is for everyone. "There is no such thing as Jew and Greek, slave and freeman, male and female" (Gal. 3:26-29). The *agape* love of God puts love where it does not find it and thus makes others lovable. The word is used about two hundred and fifty times in the New Testament, and it means sacrificial love or a love that is forgetful of self for the sake of neighbor. That is why the symbol of love is the Cross, which stands for self-giving.

Coming down to particulars, I am a Catholic because the Church believes in the sanctity of marriage and is opposed to any loosening and divorce of the bonds of love. "What God has joined together, man must not separate" (Matt. 19:6). The deep spiritual reason for the holiness of marriage in the Church is that the husband is the symbol of Christ and the bride is the symbol of the Church. As Christ took upon Himself a human nature and then corporate human natures to compose His Church, so a husband's love will no more be separated from his wife than Christ from His spouse. As a matter of fact, it takes three to make love, not two, for married love is God on pilgrimage. Duality in love leads to extinction when deliberate through the exhaustion of self-giving. Union with God is hidden in every form of human affection of husband and wife. The insatiable urges toward happiness, the anticipated ecstasy of pleasure, the constant desire to have love with fidelity, the incessant reaching for something beyond its grasp—all these constitute the mating call of God to two human souls.

Man and woman are a complementary pair—they fit together like lock and key, violin and bow. The unity between them is not just sexual but the broader unity of body and mind and spirit; it demands even eyes that can look into one another and read devotion, ears that can hear words of affection, minds that share the same truth, and tears that run down just one pair of cheeks.

I am a Catholic because I love the Church's doctrine of purity. Purity is not something negative but positive: a reverence for the mystery of creativeness that will suffer no schism between the use of the power to beget and its divinely ordained purpose. The pure would no more think of isolating the capacity to share in God's creativeness than they would think of using a knife, apart from its purpose, to stab a neighbor. The physical aspect which is sex is never alienated from the invisible mysterious counterpart which is hidden from everyone except those whose lives are committed to share in God's purpose in marriage.

The Church is opposed to fornication because it is a divorce of sex and the will. The essence of obscenity is the turning of an inner mystery into a jest, like stomping on the American flag. Purity is psychical before it is physical; it is first in the mind and heart and then overflows to the body. Purity is a reverent inwardness, not biological intactness. It is not something private, but rather something secret which is not to be "told" until it is God-approved.

Purity is a consciousness that each person possesses a gift which can be given only once and can be received only once. In the unity of flesh he makes her a woman; she makes him a man. They may enjoy the gift many times, but once given it cannot be taken back either in man or woman. It is not just a physiological experience but the unraveling of a mystery. As one can pass just once from ignorance to knowledge, for example, concerning the law of gravitation, so one can pass just once from incompleteness to the full knowledge of self which the partner brings. Once that borderline is crossed, neither belongs wholly to self. Reciprocity has created some kind of dependence; a riddle has been solved, a mystery has been revealed; the dual have become a unity, either sanctioned by God or else in defiance of His Will.

I am a Catholic because I believe in the continuity of love and life. As I have previously pointed out, and again emphasize, the unity and the creative aspects of marriage cannot be separated by human manipulation. It is true that nature does separate them, for not every love relation of husband and wife results in life. But because nature separates it would be quite wrong to say that man may separate by deliberately preventing the fruits of the act of generation. Nature sometimes spreads diseases, but man may not do these things. Sex love is not meant for death. *Eros* is for *bios*. Love is for life. Hence, abortion is wrong. As Rom Landau put it, "If the ultimate aim of sex is not new life, what else can it be? There is one alternative and one alone: Death. Sexual life that has become chaotic implies both spiritually and physically a nationwide waste (killing) of the procreative potential (which means unborn children). Such a waste is identical with death."

Procreation is the sign of both the unity and continuity of spouses. A man and woman who think of the life of each as bounded by the time limits of a cow cannot wait for the future; the craving for immediate pleasure kills the willingness to plant a flower and wait for it to bloom. Only those who have immortality in their hearts really yearn to prolong that immortality through the child. An impoverished heart has nothing to contribute but its emptiness and, therefore, nothing to transmit to posterity. No one can give what he does not have. The will to stifle life is a confession that one lacks life, that the spirit has become sterile, that even human life seems worthless. If one cannot bear the ennui and boredom of his own life, there is no urge to give life to others. The denial of the offspring is a sign of the deadening of the spirit.

I am a Catholic because I believe in fatherhood. One could write a separate paragraph on motherhood, but that is already implied in the giving of life. But because of our Supreme Court decision it now becomes important to stress fatherhood. The highest court in our land has decided that it is unnecessary for a woman to obtain the consent of the child's father before she aborts—regardless of whether she is married or not. In addition to denying rights to the child, there now is a denial of the rights of the father. This brings up the question, if the father is no longer responsible for the child's existence, then should he be obliged to support the product of that union? There is no denying that the father played a part in the begetting of the child. Has a mother then the right to the complete disposal of what to her is so much human garbage, if the body is partly his body? All this runs counter to the profound psychological changes that take place in a father as well as in a mother. Maternity hospitals sometimes find it more difficult to deal with peripatetic fathers than laboring mothers. The fact is that the consciousness of fatherhood does something to a man when he is called "father." It is like priestly ordination which summons him to spiritual responsibility.

The thrill of the farmer in the springtime as he sees the grains of wheat which he planted come up through the dead earth, or the joy of seeing a geranium bud in a tin can full of earth on a tenement windowsill, or the ecstasy of a saint at seeing a sinner dead in sin responding to a word of prayer—all these are earth's witnesses to the inherent happiness that comes to anyone who sees life springing, sprouting, or a-borning. The realization that the father has passed on the torch of life and can see it flowering before his own eyes in his "own image and likeness" is the basic reason why, when he has become a father, he is no longer just a man. It is the supreme moment of self-recovery, the re-signing of the lease on life; it is time's best moment when a man feels within himself the shimmering refraction of the eternal joy of the

Eternal Father begetting a Son and saying to Him in the noontide of paternity, "Thou art My Son, this day have I begotten Thee" (Psalm 2:7).

I am a Catholic because I believe that Divine Love pardons sin.

Because man has exhausted discovery of what is outside himself, he has now had recourse to two new "discoveries" which are exhausting his interest—one is sex and the other is the psychic self. First as regards sex, the multiplicity of books appearing on the technology of sex makes it seem as if all of the previous ages which produced the generations of millions of people knew nothing about this all-absorbing subject of the twentieth century. The other discovery is the psychic self. Because it belongs to the human personality, it is felt that it is something that he himself can explore by analysis.

It is worth pointing out, however, that there is another discovery that is yet to be made, and that is the discovery of the shadow within the human personality. As the moon has its bright and dark sides, so every human nature has its bright and shadowy sides. The shadow in us is what is repressed, shameful, hidden, the things that we have done which we wish we had left undone, embarrassing situations, betrayals, infidelities, and the like. The shadow differs from the subconscious inasmuch as the subconscious belongs purely to the psychical whereas the shadow belongs to the ethical and moral order.

The great beauty of Catholicism in the twentieth century is that it takes account of the shadow and shows how it can be extinguished by light. The shadow very simply is sin and guilt. Our contemporaries do not like to hear the word "sin." In fact, it was used only once in all of the proclamations of presidents from Washington to the present and that was by Abraham Lincoln in his proclamation of 1863. It used to be that Catholics were the only ones who believed in the Immaculate Conception of the Blessed Mother; now everyone believes that he is immaculately conceived. As Karl Menninger of the Menninger Institute of Psychiatry has written, "Whatever became of sin?" Religion dropped the concept of sin and the lawyers picked it up and it became a crime; then the psychiatrists picked up crime from the lawyers and turned it into a complex in which there was no guilt. If there was, it was to be blamed on Oedipus and Electra. Man today is not a sinner, he is "sick"; he does not need to cast himself on his knees and beg God for forgiveness, but rather to throw himself on a couch and have his sins explained away at $65.00 an hour. The shadows that lurk in the heart are actually caused by repression of the light. As Aldous Huxley admitted, "I had motives for not wanting the world to have meaning, constantly assumed that it had none, and was able without any difficulty to find satisfying reasons for this assumption." God the Light is not so much denied; He is repressed; He is dismissed. Too often the passion for changing the outside world is merely an excuse for not changing self. The young want to change the world and the old want to change youth.

Christ explained this flight into the shadow: "You will not come to Me because your lives are evil." The imperial self seeks to protect itself against values that are incompatible with it. For example, the adulterer shrinks from hearing about infidelity; the thief changes the subject when the conversation turns to justice; and the bigot turns off a broadcast on religion. If a light were allowed in the dark of conscience, it would demand a reconstruction of life, which is not wanted by those who prefer the shadows. The hell reserved for the punishment of the wicked as an objective fact in Scripture was denied; then it was moved back into the mind, where the psychologists and psychiatrists did their best to extinguish its flames, but this inner hell was worse than the outer hell: When its inner flames of remorse became unendurable, hell was shifted once more outside of the human mind and began to be incarnate in our nuclear bombs. As the English poet John Wain put it, "Now from this pain more pain was brought to earth. More hate, more anguish, till at last it cried, 'Release this fire to gnaw the crusty earth.' Make it a flame that's obvious to sight and let us say we kindled it ourselves to split the skulls of men and let in light. . . . we cannot judge but we can still destroy."

What the Catholic Church brings to this shadow is, first of all, a recognition of sin and guilt. Sin is not the worst thing in the world. The worst thing in the world is the denial of sin. If I am blind and deny there is any such thing as light, I will never see. If I am deaf and deny there is any such thing as harmony, I will never hear. If I am a sinner and deny sin, I shall never be redeemed. And the second fact is that sin is overcome by the love of God in Christ, who shed His Blood for our redemption.

The basic and most profound theology of the Church sees sin not just as the breaking of a law but as hurting someone we love. Hence in the confession of sins the Church bids the penitent keep the Crucifix in view. Christ on the Cross is the autobiography of everyone in the world. Let no one say his life has not been written. The skin of Christ is the parchment, His blood is the ink, the nail or the sword are the pen. Grasping avarice is written in the pierced hands. The prodigal feet that left the Father's house are fastened with steel. All false loves are seen in the broken heart and all proud thoughts in the crown of thorns and all blasphemies on the parched lips and all evil thoughts in the crowned head. The sins that we thought were buried in the shadows are brought to light by the revelation of Divine Love. It is no outside analyst or psychiatrist who examines the mind but the penitent himself in the light of the Holy Spirit who examines his own conscience. A person can be proud of the revelation of his mind, but no one is proud of the revelation of his conscience. All the ground glass and all the antibodies that crawl into the human heart are now divulged, never to be recorded in a book written by a confessor, for he acts only as a minister of Divine Love and what he is told is told to God as an eternal secret.

In the confessional more than any other place the love of God for sinners is manifested in His Church. There our failings begin to take on their true nature—as even Freud himself must have acknowledged, for in his *Psychopathology of Everyday Life* he gives a number of examples. If we translated them in terms of the Sermon on the Mount, 57 of his examples were concerned with dishonesty, 39 with impurity, 122 with selfishness, and 42 with hate. They all belong to the ethical and not the psychical order in being violations of God's law and eventually they must be brought to Him for judgment and pardon.

I thank God particularly for being a Catholic in this twentieth century, for I believe that we are *the end of Christendom, not the end of Christianity*. By Christendom I mean the political, economic, social, and technological world as influenced by the gospel. The closest the world ever came to Christendom was after the peace of Constantine or in the Middle Ages, but even then it was far from it, for the Church can never be completely identified with the world. We are not at the end of Christianity, for Christ will be with His Church, as He promised, until the end of time. As the serpent loses its skin and the trees their leaves, so the Church is not a continuing thing. It dies and rises again, and its great deaths and resurrections happen about every four hundred years. When the Church is holy, the opposition comes from without in the form of persecution; when the Church is not holy, the opposition comes from within by the weakness of its own and especially the spiritual decline of its clergy.

The present "death" of the Church is secularization, but the Church is now beginning to rise from that false identification with the world which characterized it for a few years. Now the shadowed hearts and searching minds want a Church that is right not only when the world is right, but right when the world is wrong. In the midst of these troubled times it is well to recall a letter that St. Augustine wrote to the virgin Felice, who was disturbed over the conduct of some in the Church:

For if in the days of the Apostles there were false brethren who made the Apostles groan and complain of "perils from false brethren" [2 Cor. 11:26], and yet he did not cast them out but bore with them patiently, how much more now would he not meet with them; since at this age which draws to a close the Saviour said:

"because iniquity hath abounded the charity of many shall grow cold." But yet let us be consoled and encouraged by what follows: "he that shall persevere to the end shall be saved" [Matt. 24:12–13].

Just as there are good and bad among the shepherds, so there are good and bad in the flocks. The good are the sheep; the bad are the goats, but all feed together in the same pastures for the Prince of Shepherds shall come, even the "One Shepherd" [John 10:16]. Then as He promised He will divide as the Shepherd, the sheep from the goats [Matt. 25:32]. As for us, He commands us to gather the flock and reserves the work of separation for Himself; He only may separate who cannot err. Presumptuous servants have lightly dared to separate before the time reserved by the Saviour for Himself; and these are they who are separated from Catholic unity. All soiled by schism as they are, how can they call themselves a clean flock?

To really understand the Church, one must think of Christ living through the centuries: living in promise in the Old Testament, in the prophets and in the psalms and in the Law, living for three decades on this earth in a tiny area of space not much larger than the state of Delaware, living ever since in the Church, which is His Body. A man who is fifty today is the same person he was fifty years ago despite the changes in his bodily life and the historic upheavals of his times. So the Church is an abiding person through these twenty centuries. The only difference between her now and then is the difference between the acorn and the oak, the mustard seed and the great tree. Her members have come and gone, like cells in human bodies, but her Spirit has remained one and the same. And since it is the Spirit which makes the Body, the Church which is the Body of Christ has been contemporaneous with the centuries. When we wish, therefore, to know Christ, we go to Him in His totality in the Church, which has been living these centuries. If we but

listen, the Church would speak to us. It alone is apostolic
and goes back to Christ and this is what it says to us:

I live with Christ. I saw His Mother and I know her to
be a Virgin and the loveliest and purest of women in
Heaven and on earth; I saw Christ at Caesarea Philippi,
when after changing Simon's name to Rock, He told
him he was the Rock upon which the Church would be
built and it would endure until the consummation of
the world. I saw Christ hanging on a Cross. I saw Him
rise from His tomb; I saw Magdalen rush to His feet; I
saw the angels clad in white beside the great stone; I was
in the Cenacle room when doubting Thomas put fingers
into His Hands; I was on Olivet when He ascended into
Heaven and promised to send His Spirit to the Apostles
and to make them the foundation of His new Body on
earth. I was at the stoning of Stephen, saw Saul hold the
garments of those who slew him, and later I heard Saul,
as Paul, preach Christ and Him crucified; I witnessed
the beheading of Peter and Paul in Rome; and with my
very eyes saw tens of thousands of martyrs crimson the
sands with their blood rather than deny the Faith Peter
and Paul had preached to them. I was living when
Boniface was sent to Germany, when Augustine went to
England, Cyril and Methodius to the Poles and Patrick
to Ireland; at the beginning of the ninth century I recall
seeing Charlemagne crowned as king in matters temporal as Peter's Vicar was recognized as supreme in matters
spiritual; in the thirteenth century I saw the great stones
cry out in tribute and burst into Gothic Cathedrals; in
the shadows of those same walls I saw great cathedrals
of thought arise in the prose of Aquinas and Bonaven-
ture and in the poetry of Dante; in the sixteenth century
I saw my children softened by the spirit of the world
leave the Father's house and reform the Faith instead of
reforming discipline which would have brought them
back again into My embrace; in the last century and the
beginning of this I heard the world say it would not ac-

cept Me because I am behind the times. I am not behind the times, I am only behind the scenes. I have adapted Myself to every government the world has ever known; I have lived with Caesars and kings, tyrants and dictators, parliaments and presidents, monarchies and republics. I have welcomed every advance of science and were it not for Me, the great records of the pagan world would not have been preserved. It is true I have not changed My doctrine, but that is because "the doctrine is not mine but His who sent me." I changed my garments which belonged to time but not My spirit which belongs to eternity. In the course of My long life, I have seen so many so-called modern ideas become unmodern that I know I shall live to chant a requiem over the false ideas of this day as I chanted it over the false ideas of previous centuries. I am the abiding personage of the ages. I am the contemporary of all civilizations. I am never out of date because dateless; never behind the times because timeless. I have four great marks. I am One because I have the same soul I had at the beginning. I am Holy because that soul is the spirit of holiness; I am Catholic because Spirit pervades every living cell of My body; I am Apostolic because my origin is identical with Bethlehem, Nazareth, Galilee and Jerusalem. I shall grow weak when my members become rich and cease to pray, but I shall never die. I shall be persecuted as I have been persecuted in Russia and Germany and in other parts of the world; I shall be crucified as I was on Calvary but I shall rise again; and finally when time shall be no more and I shall have grown to My full stature, then I shall be taken into Heaven as the Bride of my Head, Christ, where the celestial nuptials shall be celebrated and God shall be All in All because His Spirit is Love and Love is Heaven.

6B